# The Dragon's Gambit: China's Bid for Global Dominance and the Western Response

by

John Shenton

# The Dragon's Gambit: China's Bid for Global Dominance and the Western Response

John Shenton

Published by John Shenton, 2024.

THE DRAGON'S GAMBIT: CHINA'S BID FOR GLOBAL DOMINANCE AND THE WESTERN RESPONSE

**First edition. September 18, 2024.**



ISBN: 979-8227111081

Written by John Shenton.

# Table of Contents

# Foreword

In the 21st century, few challenges loom as large on the global stage as the rapid rise of China, and it's bid to assert dominance in every sphere of international influence. *The Dragon's Gambit: China's Bid for Global Dominance and the Western Response* provides a detailed, multifaceted exploration of this phenomenon, offering readers a critical examination of China's strategic ambitions and the global repercussions. This book does more than recount history—it dissects China's current manoeuvres, scrutinizing the far-reaching consequences and posing urgent questions for the West's response.

From its humble origins as a post-revolutionary state under Mao Zedong, China has emerged as a formidable power, one that is rewriting the rules of global engagement. As laid out in Chapter One, the historical rise of Communist China sets the stage for understanding its modern ambitions, particularly its quest for territorial and military expansion. The following chapters build upon this foundation, diving into China's assertive military strategy, particularly in the South China Sea, where its growing naval presence has sparked international disputes.

Perhaps the most critical flashpoint in China's ambitions is Taiwan, as explored in Chapter Three. The possibility of a Chinese invasion looms larger with every passing year, posing a direct challenge to U.S. foreign policy and global stability. As Chapter Four argues, the future of Taiwan may hinge on the strength and resolve of U.S. leadership, with the stakes extending far beyond the region.

Yet, China's ambitions are not limited to military expansion. The country has demonstrated remarkable proficiency in destabilizing adversaries through less conventional means. Chapter Five addresses how China has exploited crises like the fentanyl epidemic, weaponizing both immigration flows and geopolitical manipulation to sow discord within the United States. By extending its influence through alliances with states such as Russia, North Korea, and Iran, China has created a network of support that directly counters the West's influence, as detailed in Chapter Six.

Despite its outward show of strength, China's economic foundation remains fragile, presenting the West with opportunities to disrupt its expansion. Chapters Seven and Eight offer readers a deeper understanding of how Western economic dominance, particularly in energy, can be leveraged to counter China's global ambitions and influence the shifting dynamics within BRICS nations.

One of China's most dangerous tactics in this new Cold War has been its theft of Western technology. Chapter Nine unveils how China's military has systematically stolen, reverse-engineered, and copied cutting-edge defence technologies, posing a direct threat to Western security. This chapter also outlines countermeasures that the West can adopt to mitigate this theft.

The economic battlefield is not only defined by military technology but also by currency. As Chapter Ten explains, China's long-term goal of displacing the U.S. dollar as the world's reserve currency with its own digital Yuan is more than an economic ambition—it is a bid to reshape the global financial order and cement its place as the world's dominant power.

Through these ten chapters, *The Dragon's Gambit* paints a sobering picture of the complex chessboard that defines modern geopolitics. China is playing a long game, one that requires patience, precision, and adaptability. For the West, understanding this strategy is the first step in crafting a robust and effective response. This book not only highlights the threats posed by China's rise but also offers insights into how the West can and must respond to preserve the balance of power in a rapidly changing world.

John Shenton

# Chapter 1: The Rise of Communist China: From Mao to the Modern Era

**Introduction: The Origins of Communist China**

The rise of Communist China from its humble revolutionary beginnings under Mao Zedong to its status as a global superpower has been marked by both radical internal transformations and far-reaching global impacts. Founded on the principles of Marxism-Leninism, Mao's Communist Party of China (CPC) launched a dramatic revolution that fundamentally altered the socio-political fabric of the country. Over decades, China evolved from a war-torn, agrarian society into an economic and military giant, exerting a broad and often controversial influence on the world stage.

**1. Mao Zedong and the Foundation of Communist China (1949–1976)**

Mao Zedong, the founding father of the People's Republic of China (PRC), emerged as the paramount leader of the CPC following the Long March (1934–1935) and the eventual defeat of the Kuomintang (Nationalist Party) in the Chinese Civil War. On October 1, 1949, Mao declared the establishment of the PRC, marking the victory of communism in China. His rule, however, was characterized by a series of radical social and economic campaigns, many of which led to widespread suffering and the loss of millions of lives.

- **The Great Leap Forward (1958–1962):** Seeking to rapidly transform China from an agrarian society into an industrialized socialist state, Mao launched the Great Leap Forward, which involved forced collectivization of agriculture and an ambitious push for industrial growth. The movement, however, led to a catastrophic famine, causing the deaths of an estimated 20 to 45 million people due to starvation, mismanagement, and overzealous policies.

- **The Cultural Revolution (1966–1976):** Mao's grip on power faced increasing challenges after the Great Leap Forward, and to reassert control and revive revolutionary zeal, he launched the Cultural Revolution. This decade-long movement aimed to purge capitalist and traditional elements from Chinese society, using young Red Guards to attack intellectuals, party officials, and perceived enemies of the state. The Cultural Revolution caused severe social and political upheaval, decimated cultural heritage, and left a lasting scar on Chinese society.

Under Mao's rule, China remained largely isolated from the global economy, with a rigid state-controlled system that resisted foreign influence and participation in international markets. Despite this, Mao's China sought to support revolutionary movements abroad, providing financial and military assistance to insurgencies in Africa, Southeast Asia, and Latin America, with a long-term goal of spreading communism globally.

**2. Deng Xiaoping and the Economic Reforms (1978–1992)**

Following Mao's death in 1976, China faced the necessity of change. Deng Xiaoping, though a veteran of the communist movement, adopted a pragmatic approach to governance. In contrast to Mao's ideological rigidity, Deng is most famous for his aphorism, "It doesn't matter whether a cat is black or white, as long as it catches mice." This practical outlook led him to initiate economic reforms that would transform China into a market-oriented socialist economy, effectively moving away from Maoist principles while maintaining Communist Party control.

- **The Open-Door Policy and Market Reforms:** Deng's reforms opened China to foreign trade and investment, allowing for the establishment of Special Economic Zones (SEZs) that offered incentives to foreign companies. This marked a significant shift in China's development, laying the foundation for its integration into the global economy. Deng also encouraged private enterprise, and market competition, and reduced state control over agriculture and industry, setting the stage for China's rapid economic growth in the following decades.

- **Tiananmen Square Massacre (1989):** Despite economic liberalization, Deng's government remained staunchly authoritarian. The infamous Tiananmen Square Massacre of June 1989, in which the Chinese military violently suppressed pro-democracy protests in Beijing, demonstrated the Communist Party's unyielding grip on political power. Thousands of demonstrators, largely students, were killed or arrested, and the event cemented the government's determination to resist any challenges to its rule, even amid economic modernization.

## 3. China's Economic Ascent and Global Expansion (1990s–Present)

Since the early 1990s, China's meteoric rise has been driven by its integration into the global economy, its significant industrial capacity, and its authoritarian political model, which has allowed for centralized control over vast economic resources.

- **WTO Accession (2001):** One of the most consequential moments in China's global integration was its accession to the World Trade Organization (WTO) in 2001. This formalized China's commitment to free trade principles and opened global markets to its exports. In the years that followed, China became the "factory of the world," rapidly building up its manufacturing capabilities and developing a vast export economy.

- **Belt and Road Initiative (BRI):** Launched by President Xi Jinping in 2013, the Belt and Road Initiative (BRI) has been China's most ambitious international economic project. Aimed at developing infrastructure and trade networks across Asia, Africa, and Europe, the BRI has allowed China to extend its influence over key global regions through investments and strategic partnerships. However, critics argue that the BRI is a form of "debt diplomacy," trapping developing countries in unsustainable loans and increasing China's geopolitical leverage.

- **Technology and Surveillance:** China has become a global leader in technology, with firms like Huawei and Alibaba expanding their reach globally. However, this rise has been accompanied by increasing concerns about China's use of technology for surveillance, both domestically and abroad. The development of facial recognition technologies, social credit systems, and digital censorship have made China's model of governance a form of "techno-authoritarianism," which some countries have been encouraged to adopt, raising concerns about a global shift toward surveillance states.

### 4. China's Malign Influence on the World Stage

China's rise to power has brought with it considerable influence on international politics, economics, and security. Many analysts and policymakers, especially in Western nations, view China's global ambitions as malign, particularly given its methods of asserting influence.

- **Economic Coercion and "Debt-Trap Diplomacy":** Through the BRI and other investment projects, China has extended loans and financial aid to developing countries, often in exchange for strategic advantages. Critics argue that China intentionally offers unsustainable loans, creating dependence and leading to the seizure of key infrastructure (such as ports or resources) when nations are unable to repay.

- **Human Rights Violations:** China's repression of Uyghur Muslims in the Xinjiang region has sparked widespread international condemnation. Human rights organizations have reported mass internment camps, and forced labour, and its attempt to erase Uyghur culture, which some international observers have labelled as cultural genocide. Additionally, China's strict controls over Tibet and its crackdown on pro-democracy movements in Hong Kong highlight its increasingly authoritarian domestic policies.

- **Military Expansion and South China Sea Disputes:** China has built up its military capabilities, particularly its naval presence, with aggressive territorial claims in the South China Sea. Despite international rulings that reject China's claims, Beijing continues to construct artificial islands and militarize the region, raising tensions with its neighbours and prompting concerns over freedom of navigation in one of the world's busiest maritime routes.

- **Global Influence Operations:** China's influence extends to global institutions, media, and academia, where it has sought to shape narratives favourable to the Communist Party. Through initiatives like the Confucius Institutes, China has sought to promote its language and culture abroad while simultaneously stifling criticism. Additionally, China has used its economic leverage to influence global media coverage and stymie discussions on sensitive topics, such as human rights abuses.

## The Global Challenge of a Rising China

China's rise from a revolutionary communist state to an economic powerhouse with global influence presents one of the most significant geopolitical challenges of the 21st century. While its economic success has lifted hundreds of millions of people out of poverty, China's authoritarian model, coupled with its aggressive international posture, has raised concerns about the future of global governance and human rights. The malign influence that China exerts through economic coercion, human rights abuses, and military expansion poses serious challenges to international norms and values.

## The Rise of Xi Jinping: A Return to Strongman Politics

In 2012, Xi Jinping was installed as General Secretary of the Communist Party of China, followed by his appointment as President of the People's Republic of China in 2013. Xi's ascension signalled a stark departure from the relative political restraint of his predecessors. Xi quickly consolidated power, accumulating titles and control over the military, the economy, and foreign policy. What had once been a relatively collective leadership system became more centralized and personalized under Xi.

By 2018, Xi had effectively dismantled the term limits that had constrained his predecessors, positioning himself as China's leader for life. This move marked a sharp departure from the post-Mao consensus of avoiding excessive concentration of power. Xi's leadership has been characterized by a combination of assertive nationalism, economic expansionism, and increasing authoritarianism, both domestically and on the world stage.

Xi's China has implemented policies aimed at cracking down on corruption, but these efforts have often been interpreted as purges of political rivals, consolidating his grip on power. The Chinese government has also ramped up its control over civil society, ethnic minorities, and the media. The treatment of Uyghurs in Xinjiang, the suppression of pro-democracy movements in Hong Kong, and the relentless surveillance state have drawn widespread international criticism.

**The Deterioration of Global Peace: Xi's Foreign Policy and Its Implications**

Under Xi, China's foreign policy has taken on a more aggressive and expansionist tone, creating tensions with numerous countries. The Belt and Road Initiative (BRI), while sold as a global development project, has been viewed by many as a tool for extending China's geopolitical influence. Countries participating in the BRI have often found themselves trapped in debt or beholden to Chinese political interests.

Xi's leadership has also seen a dramatic rise in military modernization, with significant investments in the People's Liberation Army (PLA), especially its naval and cyber capabilities. China's assertive stance in the South China Sea, where it has constructed military bases on disputed islands, has raised alarms across Asia and beyond. China's growing influence in regions like Africa, the Middle East, and Latin America has also sparked concerns of neo-colonialism and a shift in the global power balance.

The relationship between China and the United States, the two largest economies in the world, has deteriorated markedly under Xi. Trade disputes, cyber espionage, and conflicting regional ambitions have created an environment of growing hostility. The spectre of conflict over Taiwan, which China considers a breakaway province, looms large. Xi's insistence on "reunification" with Taiwan, by force, if necessary, risks sparking a major military confrontation.

In Europe, China's rise has caused deep divisions, with some nations welcoming Chinese investment while others express concerns over Beijing's influence. Globally, Xi's China has positioned itself as a counterweight to Western liberal democracies, aligning with other authoritarian regimes and attempting to reshape global institutions to reflect its interests.

## Conclusion: The Consequences of Xi's Leadership for World Peace

Xi Jinping's consolidation of power and installation as a leader for life represents a profound shift in both Chinese domestic politics and international relations. His rise marks the return of personalist rule to China, reminiscent of Mao, but underpinned by a much more powerful and globally integrated economy. This shift has had significant and far-reaching consequences for world peace.

Domestically, Xi's authoritarianism has stifled political freedoms, centralized power, and created a surveillance state unparalleled in scope. His suppression of ethnic minorities, crackdown on dissent, and efforts to stamp out political opposition have drawn condemnation but little effective resistance from the international community.

Globally, Xi's assertive and often confrontational foreign policy has heightened tensions. His ambitions for territorial expansion, particularly in the South China Sea and Taiwan, have brought China to the brink of conflict with neighbouring states and the United States. China's efforts to reshape global institutions, combined with its aggressive economic diplomacy through the Belt and Road Initiative, have destabilized regions and provoked anxiety about a new era of geopolitical competition.

# Chapter 2: China's Military Expansion and South China Sea Disputes

**Introduction: The Strategic Importance of the South China Sea**

The South China Sea has long been a crucial geopolitical hotspot, a vital maritime corridor linking the economies of East Asia with the rest of the world. It is estimated that one-third of the world's maritime traffic, valued at over $3 trillion annually, passes through these waters, alongside significant oil and natural gas reserves, making the region an economic and strategic focal point.

China's military expansion and territorial claims in the South China Sea, alongside its increasing naval presence, have escalated tensions with neighbouring countries, the United States, and other global powers. Despite international condemnation and legal rulings opposing China's actions, Beijing has continued to fortify its presence, making the South China Sea a potential flashpoint for future military conflict. This chapter explores China's military ambitions, the legal context of its claims, and the implications for regional and global stability.

**1. China's "Nine-Dash Line" and Territorial Claims**

The roots of China's South China Sea claim can be traced back to its assertion of sovereignty over nearly 90% of the sea, demarcated by the so-called "nine-dash line." This line, drawn by the Kuomintang government in 1947 before the rise of the People's Republic of China encircles islands, reefs, and waters that are also claimed by other countries, including Vietnam, the Philippines, Malaysia, Brunei, and Taiwan.

China's claims are based largely on historical maps, which it argues show a long-standing Chinese presence in the region. However, these claims clash with modern international law, specifically the United Nations Convention on the Law of the Sea (UNCLOS), which grants exclusive economic zones (EEZs) extending 200 nautical miles from a country's coastline. The islands, reefs, and shoals that China claims often fall within the EEZs of neighbouring countries, exacerbating disputes.

**2. Militarization of the South China Sea: Building Islands and Fortifying Positions**

In recent years, China has undertaken extensive land reclamation projects, transforming reefs and rocks into artificial islands capable of supporting military infrastructure. The most significant construction efforts have taken place in the Spratly and Paracel Islands, with China converting these small features into military outposts equipped with airstrips, missile systems, radar stations, and deep-water ports.

- **Fiery Cross Reef, Subi Reef, and Mischief Reef**: Among the most notable examples are these three artificial islands in the Spratly archipelago. Over the last decade, China has dredged the seabed, creating vast expanses of land where airstrips, hangars, and barracks now sit. Satellite imagery reveals the presence of surface-to-air missiles, anti-ship cruise missiles, and radar systems, positioning these outposts as key military nodes in the South China Sea.

- **Fortified Presence in the Paracel Islands**: In the northern part of the South China Sea, China has expanded its military footprint in the Paracel Islands, a group of atolls also claimed by Vietnam. Woody Island, the largest of the Paracels, has been transformed into a fully operational military base with airstrips, garrisons, and missile installations. This base allows China to project power deep into Southeast Asia and even into the Indian Ocean.

China has justified these actions as defensive measures, designed to protect its sovereignty and ensure freedom of navigation. However, its militarization of the region has prompted criticism from the international community, particularly from the United States and other regional actors. Beijing's island-building strategy, coupled with its aggressive patrols by both military and paramilitary vessels, has created a situation where the potential for military confrontation is constantly simmering.

### 3. The Legal Context: The 2016 Permanent Court of Arbitration Ruling

In 2013, the Philippines took the unprecedented step of challenging China's claims in the South China Sea under the auspices of UNCLOS. The case was heard by the Permanent Court of Arbitration in The Hague, and in 2016, the tribunal ruled overwhelmingly in favour of the Philippines. The court found that China's nine-dash line had no basis in international law and that China had violated the Philippines' sovereign rights within its EEZ.

The ruling was a landmark legal victory for smaller regional claimants, but its impact has been limited. China rejected the court's decision outright, dismissing the ruling as illegitimate and continuing to fortify its claims through military and diplomatic pressure. The failure to enforce the ruling highlights the challenges of international law in dealing with powerful states that possess the ability to disregard unfavourable outcomes.

### 4. Regional and Global Responses: A Balancing Act

China's actions in the South China Sea have alarmed its neighbours and spurred a regional arms race. Countries such as Vietnam, the Philippines, and Malaysia have sought to bolster their military capabilities, engaging in joint military exercises with global powers like the United States, Japan, and Australia to counterbalance China's growing dominance.

- **U.S. Freedom of Navigation Operations (FONOPs):** The United States, which has no territorial claims in the South

China Sea but insists on the importance of upholding international law and freedom of navigation, has responded by conducting regular freedom of navigation operations (FONOPs). These missions, involving U.S. naval vessels sailing close to China's artificial islands, are intended to demonstrate that the waters are international, and that China's claims are not recognized. However, these operations have led to tense encounters between U.S. and Chinese ships, heightening the risk of military miscalculation.

- **ASEAN's Dilemma**: The Association of Southeast Asian Nations (ASEAN), whose members include several of China's maritime rivals, has struggled to present a united front against Beijing's claims. While countries like Vietnam and the Philippines have taken a firm stance, others, including Cambodia and Laos, have been more reticent, often due to their economic dependence on China. This division within ASEAN has allowed Beijing to exploit regional fractures and delay a binding Code of Conduct in the South China Sea, which has been in negotiations for over a decade.

- **Quad Alliance and Indo-Pacific Strategy**: The rise of China has also galvanized new security partnerships, most notably the Quadrilateral Security Dialogue (Quad), composed of the United States, India, Japan, and Australia. While not explicitly focused on countering China, the Quad is widely seen as a mechanism to balance Beijing's influence in the Indo-Pacific region. Additionally, the AUKUS pact (Australia, United Kingdom, and the U.S.) aims to enhance military cooperation in the Indo-Pacific, particularly through the provision of nuclear-powered submarines to Australia, directly addressing concerns over China's maritime assertiveness.

## 5. The Broader Implications of China's Military Expansion
China's military expansion in the South China Sea has broad implications for regional stability, global trade, and the balance of power in the Indo-Pacific.

- **Threat to Freedom of Navigation**: China's military presence and claims in the South China Sea directly threaten the principle of freedom of navigation, a cornerstone of international maritime law. If China were to assert full control over the region, it could potentially regulate or restrict maritime traffic through these vital waters, impacting global trade routes and access to energy supplies.
- **Strategic Chokepoint for Global Trade**: Beyond its military significance, the South China Sea is an economic chokepoint. A conflict in this region could disrupt global trade, causing economic ripple effects across the world. Countries that rely on the sea for oil, gas, and other resources would be particularly vulnerable to any instability in the region.
- **Potential Flashpoint for Conflict**: The South China Sea remains one of the most likely flashpoints for a military conflict involving a great power. Tensions between China and the United States, exacerbated by close encounters between their naval forces, carry the risk of miscalculation. A minor incident in these contested waters could rapidly escalate into a broader confrontation, pulling in regional and global actors.
- **Influence over Smaller Nations**: By leveraging its military might and economic influence, China has been able to coerce smaller nations into acquiescence. Several countries in Southeast Asia, dependent on China for trade and investment, have been reluctant to challenge Beijing's claims.

This dynamic has allowed China to continue expanding its control without significant opposition from the region, shifting the balance of power in its favour.

## Conclusion: Navigating the Uncertain Waters Ahead

China's military expansion in the South China Sea is a manifestation of its broader strategy to project power, secure critical resources, and assert regional dominance. The militarization of the region not only poses risks for Southeast Asian countries but also has profound implications for the global order, particularly in terms of freedom of navigation, international law, and the balance of power in the Indo-Pacific.

While China has sought to frame its actions as defensive, its continued militarization, rejection of international rulings, and aggressive posture suggest an ambition to control one of the world's most strategically significant waterways. The challenge for the international community, and especially for the United States and China's regional neighbours, will be how to manage this assertiveness without triggering a catastrophic conflict while safeguarding the principles of international law and open maritime access. The South China Sea is poised to remain a key arena in the contest for influence in the 21st century.

# Chapter 3: The Impending Invasion of Taiwan: China's Next Move?

**Introduction: Taiwan's Strategic Importance and the Chinese Perspective**

Taiwan, an island of roughly 24 million people, stands at the epicentre of one of the most volatile geopolitical confrontations of the 21st century. Formerly known as Formosa, Taiwan has become a symbol of defiance against the authoritarian control of the People's Republic of China (PRC) while simultaneously embodying the hopes of democratic governance and self-determination in Asia. For China, Taiwan is seen not just as a breakaway province, but as a historical and cultural imperative, the "last piece" of reunification under the banner of a powerful, unified China.

Since 1949, when the defeated Nationalist (Kuomintang) forces retreated to Taiwan after the Chinese Civil War, the island has maintained de facto independence. However, it has never declared formal independence due to the threat of Chinese military action. The PRC considers Taiwan an integral part of its territory under its "One China" policy and has consistently vowed to reunite the island with the mainland, by force if necessary. The question looming over the Taiwan Strait is no longer if China will attempt to seize Taiwan but when.

This chapter explores the motivations behind China's desire to reclaim Taiwan, the military strategies China might employ, the geopolitical ramifications of such a move, and the potential for global conflict that an invasion of Taiwan could unleash.

**1. Historical Context: The Chinese Civil War and the Legacy of Formosa**

To understand China's current stance on Taiwan, it is essential to revisit the aftermath of the Chinese Civil War (1927–1949). The war ended with Mao Zedong's Communist Party of China (CPC) seizing control of mainland China, while Chiang Kai-shek's Nationalist government fled to Taiwan, where it established the Republic of China (ROC). For decades, the ROC represented China in the United Nations and on the global stage, while the PRC remained largely isolated.

In 1971, the PRC was recognized as the legitimate government of China, and Taiwan lost its seat at the United Nations. Since then, Taiwan has struggled with international recognition, with only a handful of countries maintaining official diplomatic relations with the island. The PRC's stance has remained unyielding: Taiwan is a part of China, and any attempt to declare independence would be met with military force.

Despite these pressures, Taiwan has flourished as a democratic society, with its political system, military, and economy. The island has become a major global hub for high-tech industries, particularly in semiconductor manufacturing, and has built strong unofficial ties with countries like the United States, Japan, and others.

## 2. China's Strategic Motivations for Reclaiming Taiwan

Beijing's desire to annex Taiwan is motivated by a combination of national pride, strategic necessity, and domestic politics. Taiwan holds immense symbolic value for the Chinese Communist Party (CCP), which has made reunification with Taiwan a key aspect of its nationalist agenda.

- **Nationalism and the "One China" Principle**: The CCP has long promoted the idea that there is only "One China" and that Taiwan is an inseparable part of Chinese territory. Nationalism is a powerful force in Chinese domestic politics, and reunifying Taiwan with the mainland is seen as the fulfilment of a long-standing national mission. President Xi Jinping, who has strengthened his hold on power and aligned himself with the historical legacies of Mao and Deng

Xiaoping, has frequently emphasized the inevitability of "reunification," casting it as a measure of the CCP's success and legitimacy.

- **Geopolitical and Military Importance**: Strategically, Taiwan holds a critical position in the first island chain, a series of archipelagos that stretch from Japan, through Taiwan, down to the Philippines. For China, gaining control of Taiwan would enable it to project power further into the Pacific, control vital sea lanes, and significantly weaken the U.S.'s ability to defend its allies in the region. Taiwan's location is vital for both the defence of the Chinese mainland and as a base for offensive operations that could disrupt regional security dynamics.

- **Economic and Technological Influence**: Taiwan's advanced semiconductor industry is another crucial factor. Taiwanese companies, particularly the Taiwan Semiconductor Manufacturing Company (TSMC), produce the world's most advanced microchips, which are vital for everything from consumer electronics to military hardware. Seizing control of Taiwan's technology sector would give China significant leverage in the global supply chain for high-tech products, advancing its aspirations for technological dominance.

## 3. China's Military Strategies for Invading Taiwan

China has been steadily modernizing its military capabilities over the past several decades, transforming the People's Liberation Army (PLA) into a formidable force with a focus on power projection, amphibious operations, and anti-access/area-denial (A2/AD) strategies. An invasion of Taiwan would be the most complex military operation the PLA has ever undertaken, but Chinese military planners have devoted significant resources and preparation to this scenario.

- **Amphibious Invasion**: The most straightforward military strategy for seizing Taiwan would involve a large-scale amphibious assault. This would require the PLA Navy (PLAN) to transport tens of thousands of troops across the Taiwan Strait, land them on Taiwan's beaches, and quickly seize key urban centres and infrastructure. The scale of this operation would be unprecedented, and it would depend on China's ability to neutralize Taiwan's air and naval defences, as well as to prevent U.S. intervention.

- **Air and Missile Campaign**: Before any ground invasion, China would likely launch an intensive air and missile campaign designed to destroy Taiwan's air defences, command and control centres, and key infrastructure. China's arsenal of short- and medium-range ballistic missiles, cruise missiles, and long-range artillery could be used to cripple Taiwan's military capabilities in the opening hours of the conflict. This would also include cyberattacks aimed at disrupting Taiwan's communications networks and critical infrastructure.

- **Blockade and Attrition**: Another strategy China could employ is a naval blockade aimed at isolating Taiwan from the outside world. By cutting off Taiwan's access to international trade, energy supplies, and military reinforcements, China could attempt to force Taiwan into submission without an all-out invasion. However, this strategy risks a prolonged conflict, and it would likely prompt intervention from the U.S. and its allies, who view Taiwan as essential to maintaining regional stability.

- **Psychological Warfare and Sabotage**: Beyond conventional military tactics, China could deploy psychological operations to demoralize Taiwan's population, including propaganda, disinformation campaigns, and cyberattacks targeting civilian infrastructure. Special forces units could infiltrate Taiwan, carrying out sabotage operations against critical installations and spreading chaos ahead of a full-scale assault.

## 4. The U.S. and Global Response: A Delicate Balance

Any Chinese invasion of Taiwan would almost certainly trigger a global crisis, with the United States at the centre of the response. The Taiwan Relations Act (1979) obligates the U.S. to provide Taiwan with the means to defend itself, although it stops short of guaranteeing direct military intervention. However, the strategic and symbolic importance of Taiwan makes it likely that the U.S. would intervene in some capacity.

- **U.S. Military Intervention**: The U.S. Indo-Pacific Command maintains a significant military presence in the region, with naval forces and airbases located in Japan, Guam, and the Philippines. In the event of a Chinese invasion, the U.S. could deploy aircraft carriers, submarines, and other forces to assist Taiwan. However, this intervention would carry the risk of a confrontation with China, potentially escalating into a broader conflict with global repercussions.
- **Allied Responses**: Japan, Australia, and other regional powers would also be closely involved in any conflict over Taiwan. Japan sees Taiwan as critical to its security and could provide logistical and military support to U.S. and Taiwanese forces. The Quadrilateral Security Dialogue (Quad), comprising the U.S., Japan, India, and Australia, has increasingly focused on countering Chinese expansionism,

and the defence of Taiwan could become a rallying point for this alliance.

- **Economic Sanctions and Global Impact**: Beyond military intervention, a Chinese invasion of Taiwan would likely result in severe economic sanctions imposed by Western nations. China's economy is deeply integrated into global markets, and the disruption caused by sanctions, combined with the likely collapse of Taiwan's semiconductor industry, would have devastating effects on the global economy. The impact would ripple through industries reliant on Taiwanese microchips, from automotive manufacturing to consumer electronics.

## 5. The Likelihood and Timing of a Chinese Invasion

While China's desire to reclaim Taiwan is clear, the timing of such an invasion remains uncertain. Several factors make an imminent invasion unlikely, but the long-term trajectory suggests that China is preparing for the possibility of military action soon.

- **Military Preparations**: China has steadily increased its military exercises around Taiwan, conducting drills that simulate amphibious landings, missile strikes, and naval blockades. Chinese military officials have spoken openly about the need to be prepared for a "Taiwan contingency," and the PLA has made significant investments in amphibious assault ships, missile systems, and aircraft carriers that would be necessary for such an operation.
- **Political Calculations**: For President Xi Jinping and the CCP, the stakes are extremely high. A successful invasion of Taiwan would solidify Xi's legacy as the leader who completed China's reunification, while a failure could undermine the CCP's legitimacy. China may prefer to

continue its strategy of diplomatic pressure, economic coercion, and military intimidation, hoping to achieve its goals without the need for an outright invasion.

- **International Risks**: China is acutely aware of the risks of provoking a war with the United States and its allies. An invasion of Taiwan could quickly escalate into a broader regional or global conflict, with catastrophic consequences for all involved.

# Chapter 4: Calculating the Risk – China's Potential Invasion of Taiwan under a Weak vs. Strong U.S. Leader

**Introduction: U.S. Leadership and the Taiwan Strait Crisis**

The Taiwan Strait, one of the world's most volatile flashpoints, has long been shaped by the delicate balance of power between China and the United States. For China, reclaiming Taiwan is a national and historical objective; for the U.S., Taiwan represents a key element of its Indo-Pacific strategy, maintaining regional stability, and preventing China from asserting full hegemony in East Asia. The behaviour of China, particularly in contemplating an invasion of Taiwan, is significantly influenced by the strength or perceived weakness of the U.S. leadership.

A "strong" U.S. leader is perceived as one who asserts military and diplomatic influence decisively, offers firm commitments to international allies and projects confidence that the U.S. will uphold its strategic obligations. In contrast, a "weak" U.S. leader is seen as one who may be indecisive, avoids confrontation, and is more focused on domestic or isolationist policies. This distinction plays a pivotal role in China's calculus when assessing the risks and benefits of a potential military move against Taiwan.

In this chapter, we explore how China might assess the feasibility of an invasion under these two contrasting types of U.S. leadership and the implications for Taiwan, the region, and the world.

**1. The Strategic Context: Taiwan as a Test of U.S. Resolve**

Taiwan's status is more than just a regional issue—it is a litmus test for U.S. global commitments and its role as the primary defender of liberal democracies against authoritarian powers. For decades, the U.S. has provided Taiwan with military assistance and maintained a degree of strategic ambiguity, designed to deter China without directly provoking a confrontation.

However, for China, the island's future is non-negotiable. The Communist Party, led by Xi Jinping, views Taiwan as a crucial piece in its "national rejuvenation" plan. Reunification is considered not just a national priority but also a demonstration of China's rise to great power status, capable of revising the post-World War II global order.

Any potential Chinese decision to invade Taiwan would require careful consideration of the U.S. response. Beijing would need to calculate whether U.S. leadership is willing and capable of defending Taiwan, and how resolute the American commitment to protecting the island is. The strength or weakness of the U.S. leader is thus a critical factor in China's assessment.

### 2. China's Calculations under a Weak U.S. Leader

When assessing the potential for action under what it perceives as a weak U.S. leader, China may see an opportunity to act more aggressively in pursuing its ambitions in the Taiwan Strait. Several factors may influence China's thinking:

- **Perception of U.S. Isolationism**: A weak U.S. leader, especially one focused on domestic concerns or pursuing an isolationist foreign policy, may lead China to believe that the U.S. is unwilling to engage in a distant conflict over Taiwan. If China believes the U.S. is withdrawing from global leadership or reducing its commitments in Asia, Beijing could interpret this as an open door to launch an invasion without significant pushback. This was the case in historical precedents, such as in 1950 when North Korea invaded South Korea, partly due to perceived ambivalence from the U.S. regarding East Asian security.

- **Diplomatic Hesitation and Lack of Clear Red Lines**: Weak U.S. leadership might lead to ambiguity in Washington's stance on Taiwan, particularly if the administration fails to make strong public declarations of support for Taiwan or hesitates in military posturing. China may interpret mixed signals or vague commitments as a sign that the U.S. will not intervene in a meaningful way, allowing Beijing to proceed with military action at a lower risk of international escalation.

- **Domestic Political Distraction**: A U.S. leader bogged down by domestic crises—whether economic, political, or social—may provide China with the window of opportunity it needs. In such a scenario, China might believe the U.S. government would be too distracted to respond to a Taiwan crisis with the necessary focus, allowing China to invade and consolidate control before the U.S. can mobilize its forces.

- **Slow and Cautious Military Response**: A weak U.S. leader might be more hesitant to commit military forces to a potential conflict, fearing the political backlash of American casualties or an extended war in Asia. In such cases, China may expect the U.S. response to be limited to diplomatic efforts, sanctions, or military aid to Taiwan rather than a direct intervention. Beijing could anticipate that by the time the U.S. begins to act, it will already have achieved its objectives on the ground.

- **Erosion of International Alliances**: China could further gamble that a weak U.S. leader would struggle to rally international allies to Taiwan's defence. If U.S. leadership appears fractured or indecisive, China may assume that key allies like Japan, South Korea, and Australia would hesitate to act, fearing the absence of strong U.S. backing. This would significantly reduce the risks of broader international intervention and embolden China's strategic calculations.

### 3. China's Calculations under a Strong U.S. Leader

In contrast, China's approach to Taiwan under a strong U.S. leader would be far more cautious and calculated, as the risks of miscalculation could lead to severe consequences, including direct military confrontation with the United States.

- **Clear Deterrence and Red Lines**: A strong U.S. leader would be expected to draw unmistakable red lines, making it clear that any Chinese military action against Taiwan would result in a robust U.S. response. This could include direct military intervention, as well as economic sanctions that would cripple China's economy. China's military planners would be forced to consider the potential consequences of drawing the U.S. into a war, which could extend beyond the Taiwan Strait and involve other regional actors, complicating China's objectives.

- **Rapid U.S. Military Mobilization**: A strong U.S. leader is more likely to respond swiftly and decisively to any threat to Taiwan. China would have to factor in the rapid deployment of U.S. naval and air forces to the region, as well as the potential for U.S. military forces already stationed in Japan, South Korea, and Guam to be used in defensive operations. Such a scenario would increase the likelihood of a protracted and costly conflict, one that China may not be fully prepared to sustain.

- **International Coalition Building**: A U.S. leader who demonstrates strong leadership is more likely to galvanize international support for Taiwan. Allies in Asia and Europe, including Japan, Australia, and NATO members, could be rallied to provide military, economic, and diplomatic support to counter China's aggression. China would have to contend with the possibility of facing a united front of global powers, which could impose devastating sanctions, disrupt China's trade, and erode Beijing's diplomatic standing on the world stage.

- **Economic Consequences**: A strong U.S. leader would also be more willing to employ economic warfare in response to Chinese aggression. The U.S. could impose sanctions that would freeze Chinese assets abroad, cut off access to critical technologies, and restrict trade. Given China's reliance on global markets for its economic stability, the risk of severe economic backlash could outweigh the benefits of seizing Taiwan by force.

- **Strategic Patience and Long-Term View**: Under a strong U.S. leader, China might take a more cautious approach, opting for a long-term strategy rather than immediate military action. Beijing could focus on building its military capabilities, strengthening its economic and political influence over Taiwan, and waiting for more favourable conditions—perhaps a future U.S. administration that appears weaker or more willing to negotiate. This strategic patience would allow China to avoid the high risks of an immediate confrontation while continuing to apply pressure on Taiwan through diplomatic, economic, and military means.

### 4. Historical Precedents: China's Caution in the Face of Strong U.S. Leadership

Throughout modern history, China has displayed a cautious approach when confronted by strong U.S. leadership. The Korean War serves as an example of China's willingness to intervene militarily when it perceives weakness or distraction on the part of the U.S., but also of its willingness to back down when facing overwhelming U.S. forces.

More recently, in 1996, during the Third Taiwan Strait Crisis, China conducted missile tests in the waters around Taiwan, attempting to intimidate the island ahead of its first democratic presidential election. However, the U.S., under President Bill Clinton, responded by deploying two aircraft carrier battle groups to the region, signalling its resolve to defend Taiwan. China quickly de-escalated, demonstrating its recognition of U.S. military superiority and the risks of confrontation.

This historical precedent shows that China can back down when it perceives the U.S. as being committed and resolute in its defence of Taiwan. A strong U.S. leader can effectively deter Chinese aggression by making the costs of invasion too high for Beijing to bear.

## 5. Conclusion: The Balance of Power and the Importance of U.S. Leadership

China's calculations regarding a potential invasion of Taiwan are deeply influenced by the strength or weakness of U.S. leadership. A weak U.S. leader, distracted by domestic issues or pursuing an isolationist foreign policy, may tempt Beijing to act more aggressively, believing that the risks of U.S. intervention are minimal. On the other hand, a strong U.S. leader who projects confidence builds international coalitions and demonstrates a willingness to defend Taiwan could significantly deter Chinese action.

The stakes are incredibly high for both the U.S. and China in this geopolitical contest. Taiwan's future will likely be shaped by the relative strength of U.S. leadership in the coming decades, and China's actions will hinge on whether it perceives an opportunity to strike.

# Chapter 5: China's Role in the Destabilization of the United States – The Fentanyl Crisis, Immigration, and Geopolitical Manipulation

**Introduction: Hybrid Warfare and Asymmetric Strategies**

In the 21st century, the methods of warfare and geopolitical competition have expanded far beyond traditional military confrontations. Powerful states now employ a variety of tactics that include cyberattacks, economic coercion, disinformation campaigns, and the exploitation of internal societal vulnerabilities in rival nations. These are elements of what is often called "hybrid warfare" or "grey zone tactics," which allow adversaries to undermine each other without engaging in overt military conflict. In this context, China's potential role in the destabilization of the United States through indirect means has come under increasing scrutiny.

While the U.S. and China are economically interdependent and cooperate on some global issues, they remain locked in a strategic rivalry for global influence. The U.S. views China's rise with concern, particularly under the leadership of President Xi Jinping, whose ambitions for global dominance, military expansion, and control over key industries represent a direct challenge to the current world order. In response, China has adopted a variety of tactics to weaken its rival, using indirect means to destabilize the United States internally while expanding its global power.

This chapter examines how China may be playing a role in key destabilizing factors within the U.S., particularly the fentanyl crisis, illegal immigration, and other disruptive elements. While China's involvement may not always be overt, the country's actions and how they intersect with U.S. vulnerabilities suggest a pattern of strategic influence.

## 1. The Fentanyl Crisis: China's Involvement in a Deadly Epidemic

One of the most pressing and lethal crises facing the United States today is the opioid epidemic, and fentanyl lies at the heart of this public health catastrophe. Fentanyl, a synthetic opioid that is 50 to 100 times more potent than morphine, has become a leading cause of overdose deaths in the U.S. Most of the fentanyl found in the U.S. is either produced in China or relies on precursor chemicals manufactured there before being trafficked into the U.S. through Mexico.

- **China as a Major Producer of Fentanyl and Its Precursors**: For years, China was the primary source of illicit fentanyl shipped directly to the U.S. through international mail or hidden in legitimate goods. In 2019, under U.S. pressure, China officially classified all fentanyl-related substances as controlled substances, restricting their production and export. However, the flow of fentanyl did not stop. Instead, Chinese chemical companies began exporting precursor chemicals, which are used to synthesize fentanyl, to Mexico. From there, Mexican cartels manufacture the finished product and smuggle it into the U.S. This indirect supply chain allows China to continue profiting from the illicit drug trade while maintaining plausible deniability regarding its role in the fentanyl crisis.

- **Destabilization by Drug Addiction**: The influx of fentanyl into the U.S. has had devastating consequences, contributing to a dramatic rise in overdose deaths and fuelling a public health emergency. Beyond the human toll, the opioid epidemic weakens U.S. society by straining healthcare systems, increasing crime rates, and creating long-term social and economic instability. Some analysts argue that this crisis, exacerbated by Chinese fentanyl, is part of a larger effort by

China to destabilize the U.S. from within, attacking its societal foundation without ever firing a shot. The sheer volume of fentanyl entering the U.S. from China and the persistence of the drug trade despite efforts to curb it raises questions about whether this is simply a matter of criminal enterprise or if there is a more strategic, state-sanctioned dimension to it.

## 2. Illegal Immigration and the Weaponization of Border Instability

Another major issue contributing to U.S. instability is the immigration crisis along the southern border, where tens of thousands of migrant's cross into the country illegally each month. While the focus is often on the role of Mexico and Central American nations in this crisis, there is growing evidence that China may be playing a subtle but significant role in exacerbating border instability.

- **China's Role in Human Trafficking Networks**: Chinese nationals are increasingly being found among the groups of migrants attempting to cross into the U.S. via the southern border. Human trafficking organizations have developed sophisticated networks that transport Chinese citizens to Latin America, where they attempt to enter the U.S. illegally. While the scale of Chinese migration is smaller than that of migrants from Latin America, it raises questions about China's involvement in encouraging or facilitating illegal immigration as a means of undermining U.S. border security.
- **Economic and Social Burdens**: The mass influx of migrants, including those trafficked by Chinese networks, puts a significant strain on U.S. resources, especially in border states. This exacerbates already tense political debates over immigration, welfare systems, and national security. If China

is involved in enabling or profiting from these human trafficking operations, it could be seen as part of a larger effort to destabilize the U.S. by overwhelming its social systems and inflaming political divisions.

- **Potential for Intelligence Operations**: Chinese nationals entering the U.S. illegally could also represent a broader security concern. While many may be economic migrants seeking a better life, the possibility exists that some could be involved in espionage or other intelligence-gathering activities. The Chinese government has a long history of deploying non-traditional means of espionage, including exploiting migration and diaspora communities. The U.S. must remain vigilant about the potential for Chinese intelligence assets to exploit the porous border to infiltrate the country.

### 3. Cyberattacks and Disinformation Campaigns: Exploiting America's Divisions

In addition to physical destabilization, China has been implicated in a range of cyberattacks and disinformation campaigns aimed at sowing discord within the U.S. and weakening its institutions.

- **Cyberattacks on U.S. Infrastructure**: Over the past decade, Chinese state-sponsored hackers have conducted numerous cyberattacks against U.S. institutions, including government agencies, corporations, and critical infrastructure. These attacks not only aim to steal intellectual property and sensitive information but also to undermine confidence in U.S. cybersecurity capabilities. In some cases, cyberattacks can disrupt essential services, as seen in attacks on American utilities, transportation networks, and financial systems. Such disruptions have the potential to create widespread economic and social instability.

- **Disinformation and Influence Operations**: China has also been accused of conducting disinformation campaigns aimed at manipulating public opinion in the U.S. and exacerbating existing political and social divisions. Using social media platforms, bots, and fake news, China can amplify divisive issues such as race relations, immigration, and the handling of the COVID-19 pandemic, deepening rifts in American society. These influence operations are often subtle, making it difficult for the public to discern their origin, but their cumulative effect is the erosion of trust in democratic institutions and the media. This type of psychological warfare seeks to weaken the U.S. from within by polarizing its population and creating a sense of internal chaos.

### 4. China's Strategic Intentions: A War of Attrition on American Stability

China's possible role in these destabilizing factors may be part of a broader strategy to weaken the United States incrementally, using indirect means that are difficult to trace or confront directly. This kind of "war of attrition" seeks to exhaust U.S. resources, undermine its social cohesion, and distract its leadership from focusing on the larger geopolitical rivalry with China.

- **Hybrid Warfare**: China's actions align with the concept of hybrid warfare, in which military force is only one component of a multifaceted approach to weakening an adversary. By utilizing drug trafficking, immigration flows, cyberattacks, and disinformation, China can avoid direct military confrontation with the U.S. while still achieving strategic objectives. This allows China to gradually erode U.S. strength without provoking an international crisis that might draw a military response.

- **Distraction and Division**: By fuelling crises like the fentanyl epidemic and immigration challenges, China can keep the U.S. government and public distracted from more significant geopolitical issues. As the U.S. grapples with internal instability, China can continue to expand its influence in the Indo-Pacific, increase its military presence in contested areas such as the South China Sea, and pursue its ambitions for technological and economic dominance. A destabilized U.S. is less able to project power internationally, giving China a freer hand to assert itself on the world stage.

- **Economic Leverage**: China's ability to destabilize the U.S. is also tied to its economic leverage. The U.S. is deeply dependent on China for the supply of goods, particularly in critical industries such as electronics, pharmaceuticals, and rare earth elements. By controlling the flow of these goods, China could exert pressure on the U.S. economy at moments of vulnerability, compounding the effects of internal instability.

## 5. The Path Forward: Defending Against Indirect Threats

Recognizing the potential role that China plays in the destabilization of the U.S. is the first step in countering these challenges. Addressing this multifaceted threat will require a comprehensive approach that includes tightening border security, reducing the supply of fentanyl, strengthening cybersecurity, and increasing public awareness of disinformation campaigns.

- **Strengthening Border Control and Immigration Policy**: The U.S. must enhance its efforts to disrupt human trafficking networks, including those involving Chinese nationals. A more robust and coordinated approach to immigration policy, coupled with improved intelligence-sharing between the U.S. and its Latin American partners, can help stem the flow of illegal immigration.

- **Combating the Fentanyl Crisis**: The U.S. needs to continue its diplomatic efforts to pressure China into cracking down on the production and export of fentanyl precursors. At the same time, with domestic policies aimed at reducing opioid addiction and increasing the fight against fentanyl, innovation is key. Utilizing new technologies and data-driven approaches can help identify trends in fentanyl use and distribution, allowing for more targeted interventions. For example, predictive analytics can help law enforcement anticipate where fentanyl is likely to be trafficked, while public health agencies can use real-time data to deploy resources to areas experiencing spikes in overdose deaths.
- Cross-sector collaboration is equally critical. The fentanyl crisis intersects with issues of mental health, housing insecurity, and economic inequality, requiring a coordinated response across government agencies, healthcare systems, and non-profit organizations. The federal government should create a dedicated task force to facilitate collaboration between law enforcement, public health officials, addiction specialists, and community leaders, ensuring that efforts to combat the fentanyl crisis are comprehensive and cohesive.
- **Conclusion**
- The fentanyl crisis is a complex and multifaceted challenge that demands both immediate action and long-term strategic thinking. Combating this epidemic requires a balanced approach—one that addresses the international supply chain of fentanyl precursors expands access to addiction treatment, strengthens prevention efforts, reforms law enforcement practices, and embraces innovative policy solutions. Only

through a concerted, multi-pronged effort can the U.S. hope to stem the tide of fentanyl-related deaths and safeguard the health and well-being of its citizens.

- The stakes could not be higher. Fentanyl is not just a public health crisis; it is a national emergency that threatens the very fabric of communities across the country. Bold leadership, creative policymaking, and unwavering commitment are needed to turn the tide and ultimately save lives.

# Chapter 6: China's Strategic Manoeuvring – Supporting Russia, North Korea, and Iran in the Contest Against the U.S. and the West

**Introduction: A New Axis of Authoritarianism**

As China rises as a global superpower, its geopolitical ambitions have become increasingly apparent. No longer content to operate within the traditional boundaries of diplomacy and economic influence, China has actively sought to reshape the international order by forging alliances with nations that challenge the dominance of the West—namely, Russia, North Korea, and Iran. These nations share a common goal: to weaken U.S. influence, undermine Western liberal democracies, and promote a multipolar world where authoritarian regimes hold greater sway.

While China's relations with these countries vary in nature—Russia as a strategic partner, North Korea as a rogue state, and Iran as an anti-Western revolutionary regime—each relationship serves a distinct purpose in Beijing's broader strategy. By supporting these nations, China is creating a network of partners that challenge Western norms, further destabilize the global order, and help China achieve its long-term goals of reducing U.S. power and expanding its influence.

This chapter explores how China is furthering its global ambitions by supporting Russia, North Korea, and Iran, examining how these partnerships complicate U.S. and Western efforts to maintain global stability, project power, and defend democratic values.

**1. Russia: Strategic Partnership in an Era of Confrontation**

The China-Russia relationship is perhaps the most significant of these partnerships, especially as both countries are increasingly aligned in their opposition to Western influence. While their cooperation has deepened in recent years, it is their mutual disdain for U.S. global leadership and their desire to challenge the liberal international order that truly unites them.

- **The Ukraine War: A Testing Ground for Sino-Russian Solidarity**: Russia's invasion of Ukraine in 2022 marked a turning point in the global geopolitical landscape. While much of the world condemned Russia's aggression, China refrained from criticizing Moscow, instead opting to offer diplomatic support and maintain economic ties with Russia. China has provided Russia with a lifeline in the face of Western sanctions, continuing to purchase Russian oil and gas, thus softening the economic blow to Moscow. While Beijing has not provided direct military aid to Russia's war effort, it has offered indirect assistance, such as dual-use technologies and financial support that allow Russia to weather the economic storm.
- **Energy and Economic Cooperation**: Russia's pivot to China following its estrangement from Europe has been a boon for Beijing. China is now Russia's largest trading partner and the two countries have expanded their cooperation in key sectors such as energy, infrastructure, and defence. This partnership is mutually beneficial: Russia gains an economic lifeline, while China secures access to vast energy resources and strengthens its position as a global economic powerhouse. By supporting Russia economically, China ensures that its strategic partner remains viable and continues to challenge Western dominance, particularly in Europe.
- **A Joint Challenge to Western Institutions**: Beyond the Ukraine conflict, China and Russia have increasingly coordinated their efforts to undermine Western-led

institutions, such as NATO and the European Union. Both countries have pushed for the creation of alternative institutions, such as the Shanghai Cooperation Organization (SCO) and BRICS, where they exert greater influence and can promote their authoritarian governance models. This alliance is reshaping global power dynamics, offering non-Western countries a path that deviates from Western democratic norms.

China's tacit support for Russia's aggressive actions against Ukraine signals a broader alignment in their foreign policy goals: to weaken the U.S.-led international order, fragment Western alliances, and reduce the West's ability to project power globally. By backing Russia, China is positioning itself as a leader of a new bloc of nations that challenge the existing global order.

**2. North Korea: A Proxy for Disruption in the Indo-Pacific**

While China's relationship with North Korea is far more complex than its partnership with Russia, Beijing's support for Pyongyang plays a key role in its regional strategy to counter U.S. influence in the Indo-Pacific. North Korea, with its unpredictable leadership and nuclear ambitions, serves as both a destabilizing force and a strategic tool for China.

- **Buffer State and Strategic Leverage**: China views North Korea as a critical buffer state that separates it from U.S.-allied South Korea, where tens of thousands of U.S. troops are stationed. As such, maintaining stability on the Korean Peninsula is a priority for Beijing. However, North Korea's belligerent actions, including its nuclear tests and missile launches, also serve China's interests by distracting the U.S. and its allies in the region. Every North Korean provocation forces the U.S. to refocus its attention and resources on managing the crisis, drawing attention away from other regional and global challenges.

- **Nuclear Brinkmanship and the U.S. Dilemma**: China's support for North Korea extends beyond simple diplomacy. Although Beijing often publicly condemns North Korea's nuclear tests, it continues to provide the regime with economic and political support. This is especially true when U.S.-led sanctions against North Korea tighten, as China has been known to circumvent these sanctions by engaging in trade and providing humanitarian aid. By keeping the North Korean regime afloat, China ensures that the Korean Peninsula remains a flashpoint of instability, limiting the U.S.'s ability to concentrate fully on countering China's influence in the Indo-Pacific.

- **Undermining U.S. Alliances**: North Korea's nuclear and missile programs also strain U.S. alliances in the region, particularly with South Korea and Japan. Both countries rely heavily on U.S. security guarantees, and any sign of wavering U.S. commitment in the face of North Korean provocations can sow doubt among Washington's regional allies. This is precisely what China hopes to achieve: by stoking tensions through its tacit support of North Korea, Beijing weakens the U.S.'s regional alliances, creating opportunities for China to expand its influence.

North Korea thus acts as both a pawn and a destabilizing force that China can manipulate to its advantage. By keeping North Korea as a thorn in the side of U.S. policy in the region, China diverts attention and resources away from its military expansion in the South China Sea and its pursuit of reunification with Taiwan.

### 3. Iran: Strengthening Ties with a Revolutionary Regime

Iran, a long-standing adversary of the U.S. and the West, has found a willing partner in China. While the two countries have shared a pragmatic relationship for decades, their ties have deepened in recent years, driven by mutual opposition to U.S. influence in the Middle East and a shared desire to challenge Western hegemony.

- **Economic Lifeline for Iran**: Iran has faced crippling economic sanctions imposed by the U.S. and its allies due to its nuclear program and its support for proxy militias across the Middle East. In response, China has stepped in to provide economic support, ensuring that Iran can weather the sanctions and maintain its anti-Western stance. In 2021, China and Iran signed a comprehensive 25-year strategic partnership agreement, in which China committed to investing billions of dollars in Iran's energy and infrastructure sectors in exchange for a steady supply of Iranian oil.

- **Energy Security and Geopolitical Leverage**: For China, access to Iran's vast oil reserves is a key component of its energy security strategy. As the world's largest importer of crude oil, China seeks to diversify its sources of energy to reduce its dependence on the U.S.-controlled global energy market. By investing heavily in Iran, China secures a reliable source of oil and strengthens its position in the Middle East, a region traditionally dominated by U.S. influence.

- **Undermining U.S. Influence in the Middle East**: China's support for Iran also serves a broader geopolitical purpose. By backing Iran, China directly challenges U.S. efforts to contain Iranian influence in the Middle East. Iran's strategic location and its role as a leader of the anti-Western axis in the region make it a valuable partner for China, which seeks to expand its influence in the Persian Gulf. Furthermore, by ensuring that Iran remains a persistent challenge for the U.S., China keeps Washington's focus on the Middle East, thereby reducing its ability to confront China's rise in Asia.

- **Military Cooperation and Weapons Transfers**: While China has not provided Iran with the most advanced military technologies, there have been reports of Chinese military cooperation with Iran, particularly in the fields of missile technology and cyber warfare. These developments further enhance Iran's ability to challenge U.S. interests in the region, from disrupting shipping lanes in the Strait of Hormuz to supporting proxy groups that undermine U.S. allies like Israel and Saudi Arabia.

In short, China's partnership with Iran is a critical component of its strategy to erode U.S. dominance in the Middle East while securing vital energy resources. This relationship, much like China's support for Russia and North Korea, is part of a broader effort to weaken U.S. influence on multiple fronts.

**4. The Strategic Implications: A Coordinated Challenge to the U.S. and the West**

By supporting Russia, North Korea, and Iran, China is building a network of partnerships that challenge the U.S. and its allies on multiple fronts. These relationships allow China to exert influence in key regions—Europe, the Indo-Pacific, and the Middle East—while forcing the U.S. to spread its resources thin in response to multiple crises.

- **Undermining U.S. Global Leadership**: China's support for these regimes not only bolsters authoritarian governments but also undermines the U.S.'s ability to act as the world's preeminent power. By aligning with nations that reject Western norms and institutions, China is positioning itself as a leader of the "authoritarian alternative," where national sovereignty, economic growth, and power projection are valued over human rights and democratic governance.

- **Creating Strategic Distractions**

China's support for Russia, North Korea, and Iran serves as a powerful tool for distracting and overextending the United States. Each of these countries represents a unique challenge that demands U.S. attention and resources, forcing Washington to juggle multiple crises simultaneously:

- **Russia and the European Front**: Russia's invasion of Ukraine has reignited Cold War-era tensions in Europe and forced the U.S. to recommit military and financial resources to NATO. While Europe once seemed relatively stable, the conflict in Ukraine has escalated into a costly war that draws the U.S. into deeper involvement in European security. China's strategic interest here is clear: as the U.S. focuses on the Russian threat in Europe, it has fewer resources to counter China's expansion in the Indo-Pacific, especially regarding Taiwan and the South China Sea.
- **North Korea and the Indo-Pacific**: North Korea's continuous missile tests and nuclear brinkmanship keep the U.S. military presence and political focus anchored in East Asia. This perpetual state of crisis ensures that the U.S. cannot fully devote itself to countering China's territorial ambitions in the region. Additionally, North Korea's provocations also strain U.S. relationships with South Korea and Japan, two critical allies in the effort to contain Chinese influence.
- **Iran and the Middle East**: In the Middle East, Iran remains a persistent thorn in the side of U.S. foreign policy. China's strategic partnership with Iran complicates U.S. efforts to

manage the nuclear threat, stabilize the region, and protect key allies such as Israel and Saudi Arabia. With China deepening its ties in the Middle East, U.S. influence in the region is increasingly undermined. Moreover, as the U.S. seeks to prevent Iran from developing nuclear weapons, it must keep substantial military assets stationed in the region, limiting its flexibility to confront Chinese challenges elsewhere.

By supporting these countries, China ensures that the U.S. is constantly managing crises in Europe, the Middle East, and the Indo-Pacific, spreading its resources and attention across multiple regions. This leaves the U.S. in a strategically vulnerable position, as it is forced to fight a multi-front geopolitical battle, with China gradually positioning itself as the dominant power in its backyard.

### 5. A Shift Toward a Multipolar World

China's support for Russia, North Korea, and Iran is part of its larger vision for a multipolar world, where no single country—namely the United States—dominates global affairs. This vision contrasts sharply with the post-World War II era of U.S.-led global leadership, where democratic governance, free markets, and human rights were promoted as universal values. Instead, China and its partners champion a world where national sovereignty and non-interference in domestic affairs are prioritized over liberal democratic principles.

- **Challenging the U.S.-Led Order**: China, Russia, North Korea, and Iran all share a common goal: to dismantle the U.S.-led international order that has prevailed since the end of the Cold War. In their view, this order has unfairly favoured the West, allowing the U.S. to maintain its dominance through institutions such as NATO, the World Bank, and the International Monetary Fund. By banding together, these authoritarian regimes are seeking to carve out their spheres of influence, free from Western interference.

- **Economic and Military Independence**: China's growing economic strength and military capability are central to its pursuit of a multipolar world. Through initiatives like the Belt and Road Initiative (BRI), China is building infrastructure and economic partnerships that reduce its dependency on the West. Similarly, by supporting Russia, North Korea, and Iran, China is encouraging these countries to reduce their reliance on Western markets and military alliances, promoting alternative economic systems and security arrangements.

- **The Rise of New Alliances**: While formal military alliances between China, Russia, North Korea, and Iran remain limited, the cooperation between these countries signals the emergence of a new axis of authoritarian states. This axis is united by its opposition to U.S. and Western hegemony, and its goal is to reshape the global order to reflect the interests of non-Western powers. Institutions such as BRICS (Brazil, Russia, India, China, South Africa) and the Shanghai Cooperation Organization (SCO) represent early steps toward this new world order, offering a platform for these nations to coordinate their policies and challenge Western influence.

## 6. The Threat to Western Democracies

China's partnerships with Russia, North Korea, and Iran present a direct threat not only to the U.S. but to the broader Western alliance system, including NATO and the European Union. As these authoritarian states work together to undermine the international order, the West faces a significant challenge in maintaining its leadership on the global stage.

- **Political and Ideological Warfare**: One of the most insidious aspects of China's alliance with these regimes is the ideological challenge it poses to Western democracies. By promoting a model of governance based on centralized control, state surveillance, and economic authoritarianism, China offers an alternative to liberal democracy that is appealing to many developing nations. This model allows regimes to maintain power without the checks and balances of democratic institutions, and it offers a pathway to economic development without Western-style reforms.

- **Undermining Western Unity**: China's strategic partnerships are designed not only to challenge U.S. dominance but also to weaken the cohesion of the Western alliance system. Russia's actions in Ukraine, supported indirectly by China, have driven divisions within Europe, as countries struggle to balance their economic ties to Russia with their security commitments to NATO. Similarly, China's economic investments in Europe through the Belt and Road Initiative have created rifts between European nations that are eager for Chinese investment and those that fear becoming overly dependent on Beijing.

- **Global Influence Campaigns**: Beyond military and economic cooperation, China, Russia, and Iran have all engaged in information warfare aimed at weakening the democratic institutions of Western countries. Through cyberattacks, disinformation campaigns, and the funding of extremist political movements, these countries seek to exploit the internal divisions within Western democracies. China's technological prowess, combined with Russia's history of interference in democratic elections and Iran's cyber capabilities, creates a potent force that undermines trust in democratic institutions, erodes public confidence, and polarizes political discourse.

## 7. Countering the Challenge: U.S. and Western Responses

The growing alliance between China, Russia, North Korea, and Iran presents a formidable challenge, but it is not insurmountable. To counter this threat, the U.S. and its allies must adopt a comprehensive strategy that addresses both the military and non-military dimensions of this emerging axis.

- **Reinforcing Alliances**: The U.S. and its Western allies must prioritize strengthening their alliances in Europe, the Indo-Pacific, and the Middle East. This includes reaffirming NATO's commitment to collective defence, deepening security partnerships with key Indo-Pacific allies like Japan, South Korea, and Australia, and maintaining a strong military presence in the Persian Gulf to counter Iranian aggression. Unity among Western democracies will be crucial in deterring aggression from China and its partners.

- **Economic Resilience**: Reducing economic dependence on China, Russia, and Iran is another key aspect of countering their influence. The U.S. and its allies should invest in diversifying their supply chains, especially for critical industries like technology, energy, and pharmaceuticals. Additionally, Western countries should promote alternative economic partnerships with developing nations to provide a counterbalance to China's Belt and Road Initiative.

- **Cybersecurity and Information Warfare**: As the threat of cyberattacks and disinformation campaigns grows, the U.S.

and its allies must invest in robust cybersecurity infrastructure and counter-disinformation efforts. This includes protecting critical infrastructure from cyberattacks, countering state-sponsored propaganda, and promoting media literacy to help citizens recognize and reject disinformation. Additionally, cooperation between Western intelligence agencies will be essential in combating the influence operations conducted by China, Russia, and Iran.

- **Promoting Democratic Values**: Ultimately, the U.S. and its allies must continue to promote the values of democracy, human rights, and the rule of law. This involves not only defending these values at home but also supporting pro-democracy movements abroad. The strength of Western democracies lies in their ability to offer a vision of governance that empowers individuals and promotes freedom—values that China and its authoritarian partners cannot offer.

### Conclusion: A Global Contest for Influence

The growing axis between China, Russia, North Korea, and Iran represents one of the most significant geopolitical challenges of the 21st century. These authoritarian regimes, united by their opposition to the U.S. and the West, are working together to undermine the global order, promote their authoritarian models, and weaken democratic institutions. By supporting these nations, China is furthering its global ambitions, positioning itself as a leader of a new multipolar world.

To counter this challenge, the U.S. and its Western allies must strengthen their alliances, diversify their economic ties, bolster cybersecurity, and reaffirm their commitment to democratic values. This is not merely a contest of military might but a battle for the future of global governance, one that will shape the trajectory of the international system for decades to come.

# Chapter 7: The Fragile Foundations of China's Economy and Strategies for Western Disruption

**Introduction: The Myth of China's Economic Invincibility**

For decades, China's meteoric economic rise has reshaped the global economy. From a largely agrarian society in the mid-20th century, China became the world's second-largest economy, a manufacturing powerhouse, and the engine of global growth. The "China Miracle" was built on a combination of cheap labour, massive infrastructure investment, export-oriented growth, and a tightly controlled state capitalist system. This transformation has allowed China to become a formidable geopolitical actor, using its economic power to expand its influence through initiatives like the Belt and Road Initiative (BRI) and leveraging organizations such as BRICS (Brazil, Russia, India, China, South Africa) to build a counterbalance to the Western-dominated global order.

However, beneath the surface of China's economic success lies a series of vulnerabilities—economic inefficiencies, unsustainable debt, a demographic crisis, and overreliance on exports—that leave the Chinese economy increasingly fragile. The global economic disruptions caused by the COVID-19 pandemic and China's authoritarian approach to managing its economy have exposed many of these weaknesses, leaving the country more vulnerable to external pressures.

The United States and its Western allies, recognizing the geopolitical challenge posed by a rising China, must adopt a multifaceted approach to contain and disrupt the Chinese economy. This chapter will analyze China's current economic vulnerabilities and outline strategies the West, particularly the U.S., can employ to weaken China's economic power and limit the influence of its BRICS partners.

**1. China's Economic Challenges: Cracks in the Foundation**

Despite its impressive growth, China's economy faces several structural challenges that threaten its long-term stability and global dominance. These include:

- **Debt and Overleveraging**: China's rapid growth has been fuelled by massive infrastructure projects and property development, much of which has been financed through unsustainable levels of debt. Local governments, state-owned enterprises (SOEs), and private developers have taken on enormous debt burdens, leading to widespread concerns about a potential financial crisis. The collapse of major property developers, such as Evergrande, highlights the fragility of China's debt-laden economic model. This overreliance on debt to drive growth is a ticking time bomb for China's financial system.

- **Aging Population and Shrinking Workforce**: China's demographic crisis is another major challenge. The country's working-age population is shrinking due to decades of the one-child policy, while its elderly population is rapidly expanding. By 2050, China will have one of the oldest populations in the world, which will place enormous strain on its healthcare system and social safety nets. A smaller, ageing workforce also means reduced productivity, slower economic growth, and increased government spending on pensions and healthcare, further exacerbating its fiscal challenges.

- **Overreliance on Exports and Global Supply Chains**: China's economic model has been heavily dependent on exports, with much of its growth driven by manufacturing goods for global markets. However, as Western countries seek to reduce their reliance on Chinese manufacturing and diversify their supply chains, China's export sector is increasingly at risk. Rising labour costs in China have also led many companies to relocate manufacturing to countries with cheaper labour, such as Vietnam, Bangladesh, and Mexico, further eroding China's competitive advantage.

- **Technological and Innovation Gaps**: While China has made significant advances in areas such as telecommunications (Huawei) and artificial intelligence, it remains heavily reliant on foreign technology for many critical industries, particularly semiconductors. U.S. export controls on advanced technologies, particularly in chip manufacturing, have severely hampered China's ability to produce cutting-edge technologies. This technology gap threatens China's ambitions of becoming a global leader in high-tech industries and limits its ability to compete with the West in critical sectors.

- **State-Controlled Economy and Inefficiencies**: China's state capitalist system, where the government maintains tight control over key industries and financial institutions, has led to widespread inefficiencies. State-owned enterprises often operate at a loss or are propped up by government subsidies, leading to misallocation of resources. This centralization of power also stifles innovation and entrepreneurship, as private companies often struggle to compete with state-backed enterprises. Furthermore, China's centralized economic control allows for fewer market corrections, leaving the economy more vulnerable to systemic shocks.

## 2. The BRICS Partnership: A Mixed Blessing for China

China's economic influence extends beyond its borders, particularly through its leadership role in BRICS. Originally conceived as a grouping of emerging economies with the potential to challenge Western dominance, BRICS has increasingly become a platform for China to exert influence over other developing nations. However, the BRICS partnership is not without its challenges, particularly as the interests of its members often diverge:

- **Brazil**: As the largest economy in Latin America, Brazil plays a crucial role in BRICS. However, its relationship with China is complicated by concerns over trade imbalances and the dominance of Chinese manufacturing, which has hurt Brazilian industry. Furthermore, Brazil's close ties to the U.S. make it unlikely to fully align with China's geopolitical ambitions.

- **Russia**: While China and Russia share a strategic partnership, their economic relationship is largely one-sided, with China benefiting more from Russian energy exports than Russia gains from China's investment. Sanctions on Russia following its invasion of Ukraine have also limited the effectiveness of this partnership, with Russia increasingly dependent on China's economic support. However, Russia's isolation from Western markets has pushed it closer to China, potentially turning it into a long-term economic liability for Beijing.

- **India**: India, with its rapidly growing economy and strategic rivalry with China, is both a partner and a competitor within BRICS. While India benefits from BRICS cooperation, particularly in areas such as trade and investment, its ongoing border disputes and geopolitical competition with China in the Indo-Pacific region complicate the relationship. India is also increasingly aligning itself with the West, particularly through its participation in the Quad alliance (along with the U.S., Japan, and Australia), which seeks to counter Chinese influence in Asia.

- **South Africa**: South Africa's economy is the smallest in the BRICS group, and its role is largely symbolic. While China has invested heavily in South Africa's infrastructure and energy sectors, the economic benefits of BRICS membership for South Africa have been limited. Additionally, South Africa's political instability and slow economic growth make it a less reliable partner for China's global ambitions.

While China leads the BRICS coalition, the divergent interests of its members mean that BRICS is far from a cohesive bloc. This fragmentation presents an opportunity for the U.S. and its allies to disrupt China's attempts to build a unified front against the West.

**3. Strategies for Disrupting China's Economy and Weakening BRICS**

To counter China's economic rise and its efforts to use BRICS as a tool for challenging Western dominance, the U.S. and its allies must adopt a proactive strategy. This strategy should target China's economic vulnerabilities while simultaneously undermining its influence over its BRICS partners.

- **1. Diversify Global Supply Chains**: One of the most effective ways to weaken China's economic power is to reduce global dependence on Chinese manufacturing. The U.S. and its allies should incentivize companies to move their supply chains away from China by offering tax incentives, subsidies, and investment in alternative manufacturing hubs, such as Vietnam, India, Mexico, and Eastern Europe. By creating a more diversified global supply chain, the West can reduce

China's leverage over global trade and limit its ability to use economic coercion as a foreign policy tool.

- **2. Strengthen Export Controls on Advanced Technologies**: The U.S. should continue to tighten export controls on critical technologies, particularly in sectors such as semiconductors, artificial intelligence, and quantum computing. By limiting China's access to cutting-edge technologies, the U.S. can slow China's progress in becoming a global leader in high-tech industries. Additionally, the U.S. should work with its allies, including the European Union, Japan, and South Korea, to create a united front on technology export restrictions.

- **3. Use Targeted Sanctions to Disrupt Key Industries**: The U.S. and its allies should consider expanding targeted sanctions on key Chinese industries, particularly those that are critical to China's economic growth. These could include sanctions on state-owned enterprises involved in sectors such as telecommunications, infrastructure, and energy. By targeting these industries, the West can disrupt China's economic expansion and limit its ability to fund global initiatives like the Belt and Road Initiative.

- **4. Support Pro-Democracy Movements and Human Rights Initiatives**: China's authoritarian regime is deeply vulnerable to internal unrest, particularly as its economy slows and its population ages. The U.S. and its allies should continue to support pro-democracy movements and human rights initiatives within China and its sphere of influence. This could include increasing support for civil society organizations, promoting media freedom, and shining a spotlight on human rights abuses, such as those in Xinjiang and Hong Kong. By increasing the cost of China's authoritarian policies, the West can force Beijing to focus more on domestic stability, limiting its ability to project power abroad.

- **5. Deepen Partnerships with BRICS Members**: While BRICS presents a challenge to Western dominance, the divergent interests of its members offer an opportunity for the U.S. and its allies to weaken China's influence within the group. The U.S. should deepen its economic and security partnerships with key BRICS members, particularly India and Brazil, which have significant geopolitical and economic differences with China. By offering these countries alternative partnerships that align more closely with their national interests, the U.S. can reduce China's ability to use BRICS as a tool for its global ambitions.

- **6. Expand Economic Ties with Developing Nations**: China's influence over developing nations, particularly through initiatives like the Belt and Road Initiative, has been a key component of its global strategy. To counter this, the U.S. and its allies must offer a compelling alternative to China's economic dominance, particularly in the Global South. By expanding economic ties with developing nations, the West can undermine China's efforts to bind these countries into its sphere of influence. Key strategies include:

- **7. Build Alternatives to the Belt and Road Initiative (BRI)**: The BRI has allowed China to extend its influence across Asia, Africa, and Latin America through infrastructure projects, often leaving countries indebted to Beijing. The U.S. and its allies should develop and promote alternative investment projects that focus on sustainable development, transparency, and partnership rather than debt dependency.

Initiatives such as the G7's *Partnership for Global Infrastructure and Investment (PGII)* and the EU's *Global Gateway* aim to provide high-quality infrastructure to developing countries, offering a counterbalance to China's debt-trap diplomacy. By ensuring that these alternatives are well-funded and competitive, the West can limit the appeal of the BRI.

- **8. Leverage Multilateral Development Banks**: The U.S. should increase its support for multilateral development banks such as the World Bank and the International Monetary Fund (IMF) to provide financial assistance to countries in need, offering a credible alternative to Chinese loans. Strengthening Western-led financial institutions will help developing countries avoid falling into debt traps orchestrated by China and reduce their economic dependency on Beijing.

- **9. Promote Trade Agreements with Key Developing Nations**: The West should also focus on negotiating new trade agreements that offer preferential access to Western markets for developing countries, reducing their reliance on trade with China. For example, the U.S. could explore expanding free trade agreements with nations in Africa, Southeast Asia, and Latin America. These trade agreements should emphasize fair trade practices, labour standards, and environmental protections, offering developing countries the opportunity for sustainable economic growth outside China's orbit.

- **10. Support Energy Independence in Key Regions**: China's reliance on oil imports, particularly from the Middle East and Africa, is a critical vulnerability in its economic model. The U.S. and its allies should support energy independence initiatives in key regions, particularly in Europe and Asia. By investing in renewable energy projects, liquefied natural gas (LNG) infrastructure, and nuclear energy programs, the West can reduce global dependence on Chinese-controlled energy markets and create new economic opportunities for developing nations.

## 4. Economic and Financial Decoupling: Managing Risks for the West

While it is essential to weaken China's economic power, decoupling from the Chinese economy comes with risks for the U.S. and its allies, given the deeply intertwined nature of global trade. Western economies are heavily dependent on Chinese manufacturing, supply chains, and raw materials. A full-scale decoupling, if mismanaged, could lead to significant disruptions in global markets and harm Western consumers and businesses. Therefore, a gradual and strategic approach is necessary:

- **Gradual Decoupling from Critical Industries**: Western countries should prioritize decoupling from China in industries critical to national security, such as telecommunications, rare earth elements, pharmaceuticals, and advanced technologies. Government policies should incentivize domestic production of these key goods or partner with trusted allies to develop alternative sources. Reducing dependence on China in these sectors will enhance the West's resilience in the event of a future crisis, such as a trade war or military conflict.
- **Reshoring and Nearshoring Manufacturing**: Western countries, particularly the U.S., should incentivize reshoring (bringing manufacturing back home) or nearshoring (moving production closer, such as to Mexico or other neighbouring

countries) to reduce reliance on China. These efforts could include tax breaks, subsidies, and trade policies that promote local industries while minimizing the initial economic disruption of moving away from Chinese suppliers.

- **Diversifying Investment Portfolios**: As part of a broader strategy to decouple from China, Western investors should be encouraged to diversify their portfolios away from Chinese assets. This could involve increased investment in emerging markets outside of China, as well as bolstering domestic industries. Additionally, governments could introduce regulations limiting Western investments in Chinese companies tied to critical industries, especially those linked to human rights abuses or national security risks.

- **Coordinated Sanctions and Export Controls**: While unilateral actions may have limited effectiveness, a coordinated strategy among Western nations could significantly impact China's economic behaviour. Sanctions and export controls, particularly those targeting state-owned enterprises and industries critical to China's military and technological advancement, should be pursued in partnership with allies. By presenting a united front, the U.S. and its partners can more effectively impose economic pressure on China without opening gaps that Beijing could exploit.

## 5. Strengthening the Western Alliance and Institutional Cooperation

As China continues to cultivate its partnerships with BRICS nations and other developing economies, the U.S. and its allies must strengthen their alliances and institutions to counter China's influence.

This requires a renewed commitment to multilateralism and a focus on shared interests:

- **Strengthening NATO and Quad Alliances**: NATO, originally focused on defending Europe, is now evolving to address global security challenges, including those posed by China. The U.S. should continue to strengthen its role in NATO while encouraging European allies to view China as a global strategic competitor. Additionally, the Quad alliance (comprising the U.S., India, Japan, and Australia) should be deepened to enhance security cooperation in the Indo-Pacific, where China's military and economic influence is growing.

- **Economic Cooperation Through G7 and OECD**: The G7 and the Organization for Economic Cooperation and Development (OECD) remain key platforms for coordinating economic policy among the world's leading democracies. The U.S. should use these institutions to build a unified economic strategy that addresses the challenges posed by China, including unfair trade practices, intellectual property theft, and state subsidies. Coordinated action on these issues will strengthen the West's ability to compete with China economically.

- **Expanding Trade Agreements and Partnerships**: As China seeks to build new trade routes and partnerships through BRICS and the BRI, the U.S. and its allies must expand their trade networks. The U.S. should reconsider joining multilateral trade agreements such as the Comprehensive and Progressive Agreement for Trans-Pacific Partnership (CPTPP), which could help counter China's growing influence in Asia-Pacific trade. Similarly, deeper engagement with the European Union on trade and investment issues will be essential for presenting a united front against Chinese economic aggression.

- **Reforming International Institutions**: As China and its BRICS partners work to reshape global institutions to reflect their interests, the U.S. and its allies must lead efforts to reform existing international organizations. This includes promoting transparency, fairness, and accountability in institutions such as the World Trade Organization (WTO), the International Monetary Fund (IMF), and the United Nations. Strengthening these institutions will ensure that they continue to serve as platforms for democratic values, countering China's attempts to promote an alternative model of global governance.

## 6. Conclusion: Shaping the Future of Global Economic Power

China's current economic model is increasingly unsustainable, riddled with vulnerabilities that the West can exploit to limit Beijing's global influence. The U.S. and its allies have a unique opportunity to disrupt China's economic expansion by diversifying global supply chains, imposing targeted sanctions, and strengthening multilateral partnerships. By providing viable alternatives to Chinese investment in developing nations, promoting democratic values, and reducing economic dependence on China, the West can weaken China's position in the global economy.

However, this strategy requires a coordinated and sustained effort. The U.S. cannot act alone—it must work in concert with allies and partners to ensure that the global economic system remains open, fair, and rules-based. By carefully managing the risks of economic decoupling and deepening its relationships with key BRICS members and other developing nations, the U.S. can build a robust coalition to counter China's ambitions.

In the long term, the fate of China's economy will depend on its ability to adapt to the changing global landscape. As the West moves to curtail China's rise, Beijing will likely face growing internal and external challenges that could derail its ambitions for global leadership. The question for the U.S. and its allies is whether they can capitalize on this moment of vulnerability to secure their position in the future of global economic power.

# Chapter 8: Leveraging U.S. Oil and Gas Dominance to Counter China's Global Influence and Reshape BRICS Dynamics

**Introduction: The Geopolitical Power of Energy Dominance**

Energy is the lifeblood of modern economies, and the control of energy resources has long been a crucial factor in determining geopolitical influence. Over the past decade, the U.S. has undergone an energy revolution, driven by advancements in hydraulic fracturing (fracking) and horizontal drilling technologies. These innovations have unlocked vast reserves of oil and natural gas, turning the U.S. into one of the world's top producers of both commodities. By 2019, the U.S. had surpassed Saudi Arabia and Russia as the world's largest producer of crude oil and natural gas, positioning itself as an energy superpower.

This newfound energy dominance presents the U.S. with a unique opportunity to exert geopolitical influence, particularly as it faces an increasingly assertive China and a shifting global power structure embodied by the BRICS coalition. By increasing its oil and gas production, the U.S. can shape global energy markets, reduce China's leverage over key energy-importing nations, and weaken the economic foundations of the Chinese state. Furthermore, the strategic use of U.S. energy exports could destabilize the alliances China has carefully cultivated within BRICS and beyond.

This chapter will explore how the U.S., by expanding its oil and gas output, can leverage its energy dominance to counter China's global ambitions, destabilize BRICS, and potentially affect leadership and policy changes within China and its partners.

**1. China's Energy Vulnerability: A Strategic Weakness**

One of China's most significant vulnerabilities lies in its reliance on imported energy. As China's economy has grown, so too has its energy consumption. China is now the world's largest importer of crude oil, relying on foreign suppliers for around 70% of its oil needs. A significant portion of this oil comes from politically unstable regions such as the Middle East, Africa, and Venezuela, making China vulnerable to supply disruptions and price volatility. Furthermore, China imports large amounts of liquefied natural gas (LNG), particularly from Australia and Qatar, to fuel its industrial and urban development.

China's reliance on energy imports presents several strategic weaknesses:

- **Dependence on Foreign Suppliers**: China is deeply dependent on oil and gas supplies from countries that are either politically unstable or under Western influence. Any disruption to these supply chains could have a crippling effect on China's economy, which is highly energy intensive. This dependency also means China must invest heavily in securing these supply routes, whether through diplomatic means or by developing its military capabilities to protect its shipping lanes, particularly through chokepoints like the Strait of Malacca.

- **Exposure to U.S. Energy Leverage**: As the U.S. becomes a major exporter of oil and gas, China's ability to source energy from diversified markets diminishes. U.S. energy exports can serve as an alternative to Chinese reliance on adversarial or unstable regions. This gives the U.S. the potential to use energy exports as a diplomatic and economic tool to sway countries that currently supply China, such as Saudi Arabia and Russia, while also providing alternative sources of energy for China's key trading partners, thus reducing Beijing's influence.

- **The Costs of Strategic Reserve and Militarization**: To mitigate its vulnerability, China has been stockpiling strategic petroleum reserves (SPR) and expanding its naval capabilities to protect sea routes. However, maintaining these reserves and securing maritime routes through naval expansion is costly. Increased U.S. oil and gas production could raise the economic pressure on China, forcing it to divert resources away from other strategic goals to maintain energy security.

**2. Increasing U.S. Oil and Gas Production: A Tool for Global Influence**

By expanding its oil and gas output, the U.S. can wield energy as a strategic tool in several keyways to undermine China's global influence and challenge BRICS cohesion:

- **1. Undercutting China's Energy Suppliers**: China sources much of its energy from countries such as Russia, Iran, and Venezuela—nations that are politically aligned with Beijing or hostile to the U.S. By flooding the global market with U.S. oil and natural gas, Washington can drive down energy prices, cutting into the revenues of these supplier countries. Lower revenues would make these regimes more susceptible to economic pressure and less capable of supporting China's geopolitical ambitions. For example, weakening Russia's energy export revenues would significantly reduce its ability to fund military operations and strategic alliances, such as the Sino-Russian partnership.

- **2. Strengthening U.S. Ties with Key Energy-Importing Nations**: Many of the countries that are heavily reliant on imported energy, such as India, Japan, and South Korea, are also key U.S. allies or potential partners in countering China's rise. By increasing energy exports to these nations, the U.S. can reduce their reliance on Chinese energy markets and bolster strategic alliances. For instance, India, which has a fraught relationship with China, is a major importer of LNG. By supplying India with more affordable and reliable U.S. energy, Washington can deepen its strategic partnership with New Delhi, further weakening the China-India rivalry.

- **3. Undermining BRICS Unity**: Within BRICS, Russia and Brazil are key energy producers, while China is a major consumer. The U.S. can use its energy dominance to create fissures within this grouping. For example, by driving down oil prices, the U.S. can erode Russia's energy revenues, forcing Moscow to prioritize domestic economic concerns over its partnership with Beijing. Similarly, by increasing energy exports to Brazil, the U.S. could outcompete Chinese investments in the Brazilian energy sector, weakening the economic ties between Brazil and China.

- **4. Reducing China's Leverage in the Middle East and Africa**: China has invested heavily in oil-producing nations in the Middle East and Africa, using energy partnerships to secure access to resources and expand its Belt and Road Initiative (BRI). However, many of these nations would prefer to balance their economic ties with China by increasing cooperation with the West. By offering U.S. energy exports and investment in these regions, Washington can undercut China's influence and provide alternative partnerships that are more favourable to Western interests. This would reduce Beijing's leverage over these countries and limit its ability to use energy as a geopolitical tool.

**3. The Role of U.S. LNG: A Game Changer in Global Energy Markets**

Liquefied natural gas (LNG) is a key factor in the U.S. energy equation, and its importance will only grow as global demand for cleaner energy sources increases. The U.S. is now one of the largest LNG exporters in the world, with vast potential to expand its market share. This makes U.S. LNG exports a potent geopolitical tool for weakening China's energy position and influencing global markets.

- **1. LNG as a Counter to China's Energy Dominance in Asia**: China is a major consumer of LNG, particularly from suppliers like Australia, Qatar, and Russia. However, rising tensions with the West, especially following China's political support for Russia, have strained China's relationships with some of these suppliers. The U.S. can capitalize on this by increasing LNG exports to countries like Japan, South Korea, and India, which are major consumers of natural gas. By securing long-term LNG contracts with these nations, the U.S. can reduce their dependence on Chinese energy investments and cut into Beijing's influence over regional energy markets.
- **2. LNG Infrastructure and Investment as Diplomacy**: LNG requires substantial infrastructure, including export terminals and shipping capacity. The U.S. should offer investment and technical assistance to nations interested in expanding their LNG infrastructure. This approach not only strengthens economic ties but also fosters long-term strategic partnerships. For instance, U.S. investment in India's LNG infrastructure would provide a stable and affordable energy source for India, aligning New Delhi's energy security with U.S. interests and reducing China's influence.

## 4. Indirect Pressure on China: Energy as a Catalyst for Domestic Instability and Policy Change

China's authoritarian regime, while outwardly stable, is deeply concerned with maintaining internal stability. Economic performance, particularly the ability to provide affordable energy and economic growth, is central to the Chinese Communist Party's (CCP) legitimacy. By leveraging energy dominance, the U.S. can exacerbate internal pressures within China, forcing Beijing to reconsider its domestic and foreign policies.

- **1. Impact on China's Economic Growth**: China's economic model relies heavily on industrial output and manufacturing, both of which are energy-intensive sectors. A sharp rise in energy costs or disruptions to China's energy supply chains would result in higher production costs, lower growth, and inflationary pressures. In an economy where high growth rates have been essential for maintaining social stability, any significant slowdown could lead to increased public dissatisfaction with the government and amplify existing discontent over issues such as corruption, housing prices, and income inequality.
- **2. Triggering Leadership Changes**: Internal instability in China, exacerbated by economic downturns linked to energy disruptions, could spark leadership challenges within the CCP. Factionalism within the party is an ongoing issue, and a major economic crisis could give rise to alternative leadership that might take a more cautious or conciliatory approach to China's foreign policy. By applying sustained economic pressure through energy markets, the U.S. could indirectly influence the internal dynamics of the CCP, creating openings for leadership or policy changes.
- **3. Forcing a Shift in China's Foreign Policy**: As China's economic woes mount, Beijing may be forced to reconsider

its aggressive foreign policy stances. Energy disruptions and economic slowdowns would likely lead to a revaluation of costly initiatives like the Belt and Road Initiative (BRI) or the militarization of the South China Sea. The CCP may also seek to improve relations with the U.S. and the West as a means of securing more stable energy supplies and mitigating economic damage. This could potentially lead to a realignment of China's foreign policy priorities, reducing its aggressive posture and making it more amenable to negotiation and compromise on various issues, including trade, regional security, and global governance.

**5. Implementing Strategic U.S. Energy Policies to Maximize Impact**

To effectively leverage its energy dominance, the U.S. must implement strategic policies that align its energy production with broader geopolitical goals. These policies should aim to enhance energy security, maximize economic impact, and support the U.S.'s strategic objectives. Key policy areas include:

- **1. Expanding Energy Infrastructure**: The U.S. should continue to invest in and expand its energy infrastructure, including pipelines, export terminals, and shipping capabilities. Infrastructure improvements will enable the U.S. to increase its energy exports and respond more flexibly to global market demands. Investments in infrastructure also facilitate greater integration of U.S. energy into international markets, enhancing the country's ability to influence global energy prices and supply chains.
- **2. Enhancing Energy Diplomacy**: The U.S. must employ energy diplomacy to build and strengthen partnerships with key energy-importing countries. This involves not only

offering competitive energy pricing but also providing technical assistance, sharing best practices, and engaging in joint energy projects. By positioning itself as a reliable and responsible energy partner, the U.S. can foster closer ties with countries that are currently reliant on Chinese energy investments.

- **3. Promoting Energy Market Transparency**: Transparency in energy markets is crucial for maintaining stability and reducing volatility. The U.S. should advocate for greater transparency and fairness in global energy markets, including through international organizations and trade agreements. By pushing for higher standards of transparency, the U.S. can create a more level playing field and reduce the influence of state-controlled entities, such as those in China and Russia, over global energy prices.

- **4. Supporting Innovation and Sustainability**: To maintain its competitive edge and bolster its strategic position, the U.S. should invest in innovation and sustainability in the energy sector. This includes supporting advancements in renewable energy technologies, energy storage, and carbon capture. By leading in clean energy innovation, the U.S. can enhance its long-term energy security and appeal to countries seeking to transition away from fossil fuels, further reducing China's influence over global energy markets.

## 6. Potential Risks and Challenges

While leveraging energy dominance offers significant strategic advantages, it also comes with risks and challenges that must be carefully managed:

- **1. Market Volatility and Economic Disruptions**: Rapid changes in global energy markets can lead to volatility and economic disruptions. The U.S. must navigate these risks carefully to avoid unintended negative consequences, such as economic instability or damage to international trade relationships. Strategic reserves and market stabilization measures should be employed to mitigate these risks and ensure a stable energy supply.

- **2. Geopolitical Backlash**: Aggressive energy policies could provoke a backlash from China and its allies. Beijing may seek to retaliate through various means, including trade disputes, military posturing, or cyberattacks. The U.S. must be prepared to manage these potential responses and maintain robust defence and diplomatic strategies to counter any adverse actions.

- **3. Domestic Political and Environmental Concerns**: Expanding energy production and exports may face opposition from domestic political and environmental groups. Balancing energy policy with environmental protection and addressing concerns about climate change will be crucial to maintaining public support and ensuring the sustainability of U.S. energy strategies.

- **4. Strategic Misalignment with Allies**: As the U.S. pursues energy dominance, it must ensure that its policies are aligned with those of its allies. Coordination with partners, particularly in Europe and Asia, will be essential to avoid conflicts of interest and ensure a unified approach to global energy and geopolitical challenges.

## 7. The Path Forward: Coordinating with Allies and Partners

To effectively leverage its energy dominance, the U.S. should work closely with its allies and partners to create a coordinated strategy. Key actions include:

- **1. Forming Strategic Energy Alliances**: The U.S. should build strategic energy alliances with key countries and regions to enhance its influence. These alliances could involve joint energy projects, shared infrastructure investments, and collaborative research initiatives. By creating a network of energy partners, the U.S. can strengthen its position and extend its influence over global energy markets.

- **2. Coordinating Energy Policies with Allies**: The U.S. should engage in regular consultations with its allies to ensure that energy policies are aligned and mutually reinforcing. This includes coordinating on issues such as energy security, market transparency, and climate goals. A unified approach will amplify the impact of U.S. energy strategies and strengthen the collective ability to counter China's influence.

- **3. Promoting Global Energy Governance Reforms**: The U.S. should advocate for reforms in global energy governance to address challenges posed by state-controlled entities and ensure a fair and transparent market. This includes supporting initiatives to enhance the role of international organizations, such as the International Energy Agency (IEA), in promoting stability and cooperation in global energy markets.

- **4. Investing in Energy Diplomacy Training**: To effectively implement energy diplomacy, the U.S. should invest in training and resources for diplomats and policymakers. Energy diplomacy requires specialized knowledge and skills and enhancing the capabilities of U.S. personnel will improve the effectiveness of diplomatic efforts and strengthen the country's global energy strategy.

**8. Conclusion: Harnessing Energy Power for Strategic Gains**

The U.S.'s expansion of oil and gas production offers a powerful tool for reshaping global dynamics and countering China's nefarious activities. By leveraging its energy dominance, the U.S. can weaken China's strategic position, disrupt BRICS cohesion, and influence global energy markets in its favour. However, achieving these goals requires a carefully coordinated strategy that balances economic, political, and environmental considerations.

As the U.S. continues to develop its energy capabilities, it must remain vigilant and adaptable to changing global circumstances. By working closely with allies, promoting transparency, and addressing potential risks, the U.S. can harness its energy power to secure strategic advantages and advance its geopolitical objectives. The path forward will involve navigating complex challenges, but with a well-executed energy strategy, the U.S. can play a decisive role in shaping the future of global power and countering China's ambitions on the world stage.

# Chapter 9: The Great Technology Heist: How China's Military Has Stolen, Copied, and Reverse-Engineered Western Defence Technologies — And How the West Can Counter It

**Introduction: A Silent War Over Technology**

In the past two decades, China has rapidly evolved from a regional military power to a global force capable of challenging Western dominance, particularly that of the United States. Behind much of this dramatic transformation is a strategy that often bypasses the long and costly processes of research and development (R&D). Instead, China has focused on acquiring cutting-edge Western military technology through a combination of cyber espionage, intellectual property theft, and reverse engineering.

This strategy has provided China's People's Liberation Army (PLA) with advanced military hardware and capabilities that rival those of Western nations, without the billions of dollars and years of investment traditionally associated with such developments. The West now faces a technological arms race with a formidable opponent, one that does not play by conventional rules. The question now confronting the United States, NATO, and their allies is how to stop further theft and prevent China from continuing to leverage stolen technologies to advance its military ambitions.

This chapter explores how the Chinese military has systematically copied, stolen, and re-engineered Western technology, saving billions in development costs, and what the West can do to stem the tide of intellectual property theft that threatens to erode its military and technological superiority.

**1. The Chinese Approach: Copy, Steal, Reverse Engineer**

China's strategy to advance its military capabilities is rooted in a state-sponsored approach that targets Western technologies through multiple avenues. While many countries have engaged in espionage to gather intelligence, China's methods have been particularly wide-ranging, involving the state, private companies, academic institutions, and individuals in a coordinated effort to close the technological gap with the West.

## 1.1. Cyber Espionage: The Frontline of the Digital Battlefield

Cyber espionage has become China's most efficient and cost-effective method of acquiring sensitive military technology. State-sponsored hacking groups such as APT (Advanced Persistent Threat) actors, often linked to the PLA or Ministry of State Security (MSS), have conducted numerous cyber-attacks on Western defence contractors, governments, and private corporations.

For example, in 2009, it was revealed that Chinese hackers had successfully breached Lockheed Martin's computer systems, stealing classified designs of the F-35 stealth fighter jet. This theft allowed China to develop its fifth-generation stealth fighter, the Chengdu J-20, at a fraction of the cost and time it took the U.S. to develop the F-35. The resemblance between the J-20 and the F-35 is more than superficial, highlighting how the digital theft of military designs translates into tangible gains on the battlefield.

Cyber espionage has also targeted naval, missile, and satellite technologies. The theft of sensitive data related to U.S. missile defence systems, such as the Patriot and THAAD (Terminal High Altitude Area Defence), has enabled China to enhance its missile defence capabilities, as seen in its HQ-9 surface-to-air missile system. The HQ-9 is a blend of Russian S-300 technology and U.S. systems, providing China with a formidable anti-air capability without the need for extensive R&D.

## 1.2. Reverse Engineering: The Shortcut to Innovation

In many instances, China has been able to physically acquire Western military hardware—either through purchase, capture, or trade deals with third parties—and reverse-engineer the systems to create its versions. This process involves disassembling, analysing, and then reproducing complex technologies.

One of the most prominent examples is China's development of its aircraft carriers. In 1998, China acquired the unfinished Soviet aircraft carrier Varyag, which was languishing in Ukraine. Over the years, Chinese engineers studied the Varyag, reverse-engineered key components, and eventually used the vessel as the basis for China's first domestically produced aircraft carrier, the Type 001 Liaoning. This carrier, while an improvement on the Varyag, still featured significant Russian design influence. However, China's subsequent carrier, the Type 002 Shandong, demonstrated how reverse engineering enabled China to improve upon imported designs and gradually incorporate indigenous technologies.

The practice of reverse engineering has also extended to fighter jets, missile systems, and naval vessels, allowing China to field advanced platforms at a fraction of the development cost that the West incurred. By reproducing and refining existing Western designs, China accelerates its technological advancements without the steep learning curve associated with innovation.

## 1.3. Exploiting Academia and Joint Ventures

In addition to cyber and physical theft, China has also leveraged academia and joint ventures to acquire sensitive technologies. Many Western universities and research institutions, eager to collaborate on cutting-edge projects, have partnered with Chinese institutions, often overlooking the potential for dual-use applications—technologies that have both civilian and military uses.

Through initiatives like the Thousand Talents Program, China recruit's scientists and researchers with access to sensitive technologies, particularly in fields like artificial intelligence, quantum computing, and materials science. Many of these researchers work in Western labs, providing China with direct access to research that can be adapted for military purposes. Moreover, academic collaborations often result in the publication of research papers that Chinese engineers can study and apply in military contexts.

Corporate partnerships have also been exploited. Many Western companies that set up joint ventures in China are required to share technology as part of the deal. In some cases, the technology transferred for commercial purposes has been repurposed for military use. For example, American semiconductor technology—critical for both civilian electronics and military systems—has been acquired through joint ventures and then used to develop China's advanced microchip industry, which is essential for modern warfare.

## 2. The Economic and Strategic Impact of Technology Theft

The economic and strategic implications of China's technology theft are staggering. Each year, intellectual property theft costs Western companies hundreds of billions of dollars, undermining their competitiveness and discouraging investment in new technologies. More critically, stolen technology has enabled China to rapidly modernize its military, narrowing the gap with the United States and its allies in key areas such as air superiority, naval power, and missile technology.

China's military advancements have not only reshaped the balance of power in Asia but have also challenged the West's ability to project power globally. In the Indo-Pacific region, the PLA's growing arsenal of anti-access/area denial (A2/AD) weapons—many of which are derived from stolen Western technology—poses a direct threat to U.S. naval forces. Systems like the DF-21D "carrier killer" missile have the potential to deter U.S. aircraft carriers from operating in contested waters, thereby reducing the U.S.'s ability to maintain freedom of navigation in key maritime areas like the South China Sea.

Moreover, China's development of advanced stealth fighters, precision-guided munitions, and hypersonic weapons—many of which have roots in stolen technologies—has eroded the West's qualitative edge. The ability to quickly deploy these systems into production has allowed China to field a military that, in certain respects, rivals those of Western nations, altering the strategic calculus in future conflicts.

One of the most striking aspects of China's military expansion is the speed with which it has closed the technological gap with the West. Many of the PLA's most advanced platforms bear a striking resemblance to their Western counterparts, both in design and capability. Several high-profile examples highlight how China's military development has benefited from stolen or copied Western technologies:

- **1. The J-20 Stealth Fighter**: China's Chengdu J-20 stealth fighter is one of the most advanced aircraft in the PLA Air Force (PLAAF). It is also widely believed to have incorporated key design elements from the U.S. F-22 Raptor and F-35 Lightning II. In 2009, it was reported that Chinese cyber espionage groups had gained access to classified data from Lockheed Martin's F-35 program. This breach provided China with valuable insights into stealth technology, avionics, and aerodynamics, which were likely applied in the development of the J-20.
- **2. The HQ-9 Missile System**: China's HQ-9 surface-to-air missile (SAM) system shares many similarities with the Russian S-300 system, which China initially acquired from Russia. However, China has also been accused of incorporating elements from U.S. missile defence systems, including the Patriot missile system. The HQ-9's radar and missile guidance technology show signs of reverse engineering from both Russian and Western sources.

- **3. Chinese Naval Capabilities**: China's naval advancements have similarly been bolstered by technological theft. The PLA Navy (PLAN) has developed modern warships that incorporate advanced radar systems, shipborne missile technology, and electronic warfare capabilities—many of which mirror Western designs. China's Type 055 destroyer, for instance, appears to integrate elements from the U.S. Navy's Arleigh Burke-class destroyers and the Zumwalt-class destroyer, particularly in terms of stealth features and weapon systems integration.

- **4. The DF-21D "Carrier Killer" Missile**: China's anti-ship ballistic missile (ASBM), the DF-21D, has been dubbed the "carrier killer" for its potential to threaten U.S. aircraft carriers in the Western Pacific. While this missile is based on indigenous ballistic missile technology, it has likely benefited from a combination of stolen telemetry data, targeting algorithms, and satellite guidance systems from Western and Russian sources.

By avoiding the costly and time-consuming process of developing these technologies from scratch, China has been able to modernize its military at a fraction of the cost that the U.S. and its allies have invested in similar platforms. This strategy has allowed China to rapidly close the gap with Western militaries, particularly in areas like aerospace, cyber warfare, and missile technology.

### 3. How the West Can Stop Further Technology Theft

Preventing China from continuing its theft of Western technology will require a comprehensive, multi-faceted approach. Both defensive and offensive strategies are necessary to protect intellectual property, safeguard technological superiority, and disrupt China's attempts to close the military gap.

### 3.1. Strengthening Cybersecurity and Counterespionage

One of the most immediate ways to combat China's theft of technology is to enhance cybersecurity measures across government agencies, defence contractors, and private corporations. Advanced encryption, artificial intelligence-driven threat detection, and multi-factor authentication are just the beginning. Governments must work with private industry to develop a comprehensive cybersecurity framework that can detect and neutralize threats before they cause damage.

Western intelligence agencies also need to prioritize counter-espionage activities, focusing on identifying and dismantling Chinese espionage networks that target sensitive military technologies. This includes both cyber operatives and human intelligence agents who may be embedded in universities, corporations, or research institutions.

### 3.2. Tightening Export Controls and Foreign Investment Reviews

Export controls on sensitive technologies must be strengthened. The U.S. Export Control Reform Act (ECRA) has already taken steps to limit the export of critical technologies like AI, quantum computing, and semiconductors, but further action is needed. Coordinating these efforts with allies will ensure that loopholes in one country's export controls do not become pathways for China to acquire sensitive technologies elsewhere.

Foreign investment in critical industries must also be scrutinized more closely. Chinese investments in Western technology companies should be evaluated not only on economic grounds but also for their potential national security risks. Bodies, like the Committee on Foreign Investment in the United States (CFIUS) play a key role in reviewing mergers and acquisitions involving sensitive technologies, and similar frameworks, should be adopted by other Western nations.

### 3.3. Reforming Academic and Research Collaborations

Academic institutions must be more vigilant in protecting sensitive research, particularly in fields with military applications. Governments should work closely with universities to establish clear guidelines on foreign collaborations and funding. Research programs involving dual-use technologies should be subject to stricter scrutiny, and any foreign national working on such projects should be vetted for potential ties to state-sponsored espionage programs.

### 3.4. Enhancing Multilateral Cooperation

The West must coordinate its efforts with allies to present a unified front against Chinese technology theft. This includes sharing intelligence on cyber threats, coordinating export controls, and working together on counter-espionage operations. Multilateral organizations like NATO and the Five Eyes intelligence alliance should expand their focus to include the protection of critical technologies and IP from Chinese espionage.

### 3.5. Promoting Innovation and Industrial Resilience

Finally, maintaining a technological edge over China requires the West to continue investing in cutting-edge research and development. Governments should incentivize private artificial intelligence, quantum computing, hypersonic weapons, cyber defence, and advanced materials science. This can be achieved through tax incentives, grants, and public-private partnerships. Encouraging innovation within the private sector not only strengthens economic resilience but also ensures that the West remains at the forefront of military and technological superiority.

Furthermore, by ensuring industrial resilience, the West can better shield its strategic industries from foreign infiltration. This includes securing supply chains for critical technologies like semiconductors and rare earth minerals, both of which are essential for producing advanced military equipment. Over-reliance on Chinese suppliers in these areas presents a significant vulnerability, one that China could exploit in times of geopolitical tension. Building redundant supply chains with trusted allies, or increasing domestic production capacity, will reduce the West's vulnerability to economic or industrial coercion.

## 4. Offensive Measures: Countering China's Espionage Tactics

While defensive strategies are critical, the West must also consider taking the initiative in the realm of cyber and economic warfare. Counterintelligence efforts aimed at undermining China's attempts to steal technology should be escalated. This includes targeting Chinese networks involved in espionage and disrupting the financial and logistical operations that support these efforts.

### 4.1. Cyber Retaliation and Disruption

The U.S. and its allies possess some of the world's most sophisticated cyber capabilities. Just as China has used cyberattacks to steal military secrets, the West could deploy similar tactics to undermine Chinese military development. Strategic cyberattacks could be used to disrupt key Chinese military R&D projects or sabotage the implementation of stolen technologies. This could slow down or complicate China's ability to reverse-engineer or mass-produce Western technologies.

The West must also explore ways to neutralize China's digital espionage operations through offensive cyber campaigns. This could involve targeting and dismantling the networks of China's state-sponsored hacking groups, such as APT10 and APT41, which have been responsible for many of the most significant thefts of Western intellectual property. By directly targeting the actors behind China's cyber theft, the West can weaken China's ability to continue these operations.

### 4.2. Sanctions and Legal Consequences

Another tool in the West's arsenal is the imposition of economic sanctions on Chinese companies or individuals found to be complicit in the theft of intellectual property. Targeting Chinese firms that benefit from stolen technology, such as defence contractors or state-owned enterprises, would send a clear signal that such behaviour will have tangible economic consequences. Sanctions could also extend to Chinese entities that facilitate cyber espionage, such as technology firms that supply software or hardware used in espionage operations.

In tandem with sanctions, the West must pursue aggressive legal actions against companies and individuals involved in technology theft. Governments can support Western firms in filing lawsuits against Chinese entities and holding them accountable in both national and international courts. This would serve as both a financial deterrent and a means of seeking restitution for stolen technologies.

## 4.3. Diplomatic Pressure and Global Norms

Diplomatic pressure is another critical component of countering China's technological theft. The West should lead efforts to establish global norms and agreements on cybersecurity and intellectual property protection. Through international forums such as the United Nations or the World Trade Organization (WTO), the West can advocate for stricter penalties and greater cooperation in addressing state-sponsored theft of technology.

Additionally, bilateral pressure on China must be increased. Western governments should make it clear that the continued theft of technology will have serious diplomatic and economic repercussions. This may involve leveraging trade agreements or withholding access to critical Western markets and technologies unless China commits to respecting intellectual property laws and halts state-sponsored espionage activities.

## 5. Lessons from History: Preventing a Technological Cold War

The West's response to China's aggressive technology theft should be informed by lessons from history. The Cold War between the United States and the Soviet Union offers a useful parallel in terms of the arms race and technological competition between great powers. Just as the West ultimately outpaced the Soviet Union through a combination of innovation, economic resilience, and intelligence, it can do the same in its competition with China.

However, the competition with China presents a unique challenge. Unlike the Soviet Union, China is deeply integrated into the global economy, and its economic rise has been fuelled in part by access to Western markets, technologies, and investment. The West must therefore walk a fine line between competing with China militarily and economically while avoiding outright conflict that could destabilize the global order.

Preventing a technological Cold War with China will require a strategy that balances competition with cooperation. While it is necessary to protect Western intellectual property and maintain military superiority, there may also be opportunities for collaboration in areas where mutual interests align, such as climate change, global health, and space exploration. Engaging China in constructive dialogue while standing firm on issues of national security will be critical to managing this complex relationship.

**Conclusion: Securing the Future of Western Innovation**

The Chinese military's ability to copy, steal, and re-engineer Western technology has allowed it to make unprecedented gains in military capability, saving billions in R&D costs while rapidly closing the gap with the West. This theft has not only undermined Western economic and military interests but has also fundamentally altered the balance of power, particularly in regions like the Indo-Pacific.

However, this trend is not irreversible. By strengthening cybersecurity defences, tightening export controls, reforming academic collaborations, and enhancing multilateral cooperation, the West can effectively curtail China's ability to acquire and exploit sensitive technologies. Moreover, by pursuing offensive measures such as cyber retaliation, sanctions, and legal consequences, the West can disrupt China's technological heist and prevent future thefts.

Ultimately, securing the future of Western innovation will require both vigilance and foresight. The West must continue to lead the world in technological innovation while ensuring that its intellectual property is adequately protected from adversaries like China. By doing so, it can not only safeguard its economic and military interests but also preserve its strategic advantage in the face of a rising global competitor. The stakes are high, and the battle for technological supremacy is just beginning.

# Chapter 10: The Yuan's Global Ambitions: How China is Seeking to Replace the U.S. Dollar with Its Digital Currency and BRICS Support

**Introduction: The Rise of China's Economic Influence**

As China's global economic and geopolitical power has grown, so has its desire to reshape the international financial system, which has long been dominated by the U.S. dollar. For decades, the dollar has functioned as the world's reserve currency, the dominant medium for international trade, and the primary currency used in global energy markets, particularly in the sale of oil—commonly referred to as the **"petrodollar"** system.

However, China's ambitions now extend far beyond merely competing with the U.S. economically; Beijing is seeking to challenge and potentially replace the U.S. dollar as the dominant global currency. This chapter explores how China, with the support of its BRICS (Brazil, Russia, India, China, and South Africa) partners, is advancing its economic and political agenda by promoting the yuan (or renminbi) as a global reserve currency, leveraging digital currency technology, and attempting to reduce the U.S. dollar's influence in the energy sector.

**1. China's Economic and Strategic Rationale for Replacing the Dollar**

The U.S. dollar's dominant role in global trade, finance, and energy markets provides Washington with immense geopolitical leverage. This status allows the U.S. to impose sanctions, restrict access to financial markets, and effectively control the flow of global commerce. China, recognizing the strategic advantage this gives the U.S., has sought to undermine the dollar's hegemony to both reduce its vulnerability to American economic pressures and to reshape the global financial system in a manner more favourable to its interests.

## 1.1. Reducing Dependency on the U.S. Dollar

One of China's primary motivations for replacing the U.S. dollar is to reduce its dependency on the dollar for international trade, particularly in key areas like energy imports. As the world's largest importer of oil, China's energy security is heavily tied to the dollar-dominated oil market. This dependency exposes China to financial and geopolitical risks, as the U.S. can weaponize the dollar through sanctions or other economic restrictions.

Additionally, China's vast foreign reserves, heavily denominated in U.S. dollars, further tie its economic fortunes to the American financial system. The reliance on the dollar makes China vulnerable to fluctuations in U.S. monetary policy, trade disputes, and potential financial sanctions. Reducing this dependence is thus central to China's broader goal of achieving economic and financial autonomy.

## 1.2. Weakening U.S. Geopolitical Influence

By promoting the yuan as an alternative global currency, China also seeks to weaken the geopolitical influence that the U.S. wields through the dollar. The ability of the U.S. to enforce sanctions on nations like Iran, Russia, and North Korea is largely enabled by the centrality of the dollar in global trade. Countries that are cut off from dollar-denominated markets face severe economic consequences. China, which often finds itself at odds with U.S. foreign policy, views the replacement of the dollar as a way to build a more multipolar world order where American economic dominance is diminished.

## 2. China's Strategy: A Digital Currency for Global Trade

A key component of China's strategy to replace the dollar is the development of its digital currency, known as the **Digital Currency Electronic Payment (DCEP)** or **e-CNY**. Unlike decentralized cryptocurrencies such as Bitcoin, the e-CNY is fully controlled by the People's Bank of China (PBOC), making it the world's first state-issued central bank digital currency (CBDC). The creation of this digital currency is not merely a domestic innovation; it is part of a broader push to internalize the yuan and challenge the dollar's dominance in global trade.

## 2.1. Leveraging Technology to Bypass the Dollar

China's e-CNY offers a technological platform that can bypass the traditional U.S.-dominated financial system. The current global payment infrastructure is heavily reliant on the **SWIFT** network, which facilitates cross-border payments in dollars. However, SWIFT transactions are often subject to U.S. oversight, giving Washington the ability to block or delay payments. The e-CNY, being a digital currency controlled entirely by China, allows for cross-border transactions without the need to route through SWIFT or other Western-controlled systems.

China has already begun testing cross-border payments using the e-CNY, with some transactions conducted between Hong Kong and mainland China. In the future, China plans to expand the use of its digital currency to facilitate international trade, particularly with countries that are seeking alternatives to the dollar-dominated system due to U.S. sanctions or economic pressure.

## 2.2. The Role of BRICS in Promoting the Yuan

China's efforts to internationalize the yuan and its digital currency have been bolstered by its **BRICS** partners—Brazil, Russia, India, and South Africa. These nations share a common interest in reducing their reliance on the U.S. dollar, particularly in the context of growing geopolitical tensions with the West.

- **Russia** has been a strong supporter of yuan-denominated trade following its increasing isolation from Western financial systems due to sanctions. Russian energy exports to China are increasingly being settled in yuan rather than dollars, and there are discussions about using China's digital currency to further facilitate trade.
- **Brazil** and **India**, both rising economic powers, are interested

in diversifying their currencies in trade transactions, especially in sectors like agriculture and manufacturing. While India has historically been wary of China's growing influence, its participation in BRICS has allowed it to explore alternatives to the U.S.-led financial system.

Together, the BRICS nations have discussed the possibility of creating a shared digital currency for trade among member states, with the yuan playing a central role. This would not only reduce the bloc's dependence on the dollar but also provide a platform for the expansion of China's digital currency beyond its immediate borders.

### 2.3. The Petro-Yuan: Challenging the Dollar in Energy Markets

One of the most significant challenges to the dollar's global dominance is the potential shift in how oil is traded. The **petrodollar system**, established in the 1970s, ensured that global oil transactions were conducted almost exclusively in U.S. dollars, which bolstered demand for the dollar and entrenched its role as the world's reserve currency. However, China, as the world's largest importer of oil, is pushing for the adoption of the **"petro-yuan"** to replace the dollar in oil transactions.

China has already begun laying the groundwork for this shift by establishing yuan-denominated oil futures contracts on the **Shanghai International Energy Exchange (INE)**. This move allows oil-exporting countries to sell their crude in yuan rather than dollars, providing an alternative to the petrodollar system. Some oil exporters, particularly those facing U.S. sanctions, have shown interest in settling oil sales in yuan. For example, **Iran** and **Venezuela**, both under U.S. economic sanctions, have indicated their willingness to trade oil in yuan.

Additionally, **Russia** has begun settling a significant portion of its energy exports to China in yuan. As the relationship between Moscow and Beijing deepens, particularly amid Western sanctions on Russia following its invasion of Ukraine, the petro-yuan may gain further traction, especially if Saudi Arabia and other key oil producers in the Middle East adopt the currency.

## 3. Disrupting the U.S. Dollar's Dominance: Challenges and Opportunities for China

While China has made significant strides in promoting the yuan and its digital currency as alternatives to the dollar, the process of replacing the U.S. dollar as the world's reserve currency is fraught with challenges. The U.S. dollar's dominance is deeply entrenched, and the global financial system is built on decades of trust, liquidity, and stability associated with the dollar.

### 3.1. Trust and Global Acceptance of the Yuan

One of the biggest obstacles China faces in promoting the yuan as a global currency is the issue of trust. The U.S. dollar's status as the world's reserve currency is underpinned by the transparency and rule of law associated with the American financial system. Investors and governments trust the dollar because of its liquidity, the stability of U.S. institutions, and the strength of the U.S. economy.

By contrast, the Chinese financial system is seen as opaque, with heavy government intervention and capital controls. These concerns have limited the yuan's global acceptance, particularly as a store of value. While China has been working to open its financial markets and internationalize the yuan, many countries and investors remain hesitant to fully embrace it due to concerns about government control and economic transparency.

### 3.2. Competition from Other Digital Currencies

While China's digital currency is one of the first state-backed efforts of its kind, it is not the only one. Other nations are developing their own **central bank digital currencies (CBDCs)**, and these currencies could potentially compete with the e-CNY for global adoption. The European Central Bank, for example, is exploring the creation of a **digital euro**, and several other countries, including Japan and South Korea, are working on their digital currencies.

Moreover, private cryptocurrencies such as Bitcoin and Ethereum, though not state-backed, also offer an alternative to traditional currencies. These decentralized digital currencies are gaining popularity as mediums of exchange and stores of value, providing another potential competitor to both the dollar and the yuan.

### 3.3. U.S. Countermeasures and Global Financial Architecture

The U.S. is unlikely to sit idly by as China seeks to undermine the dollar's dominance. In response to China's efforts, the U.S. could take several countermeasures to strengthen the dollar's position. This could include improving the efficiency of the global dollar payment system, implementing its digital currency (a **digital dollar**), or developing new mechanisms to maintain the U.S. dollar's dominance in global trade. Recent discussions about a U.S. **central bank digital currency (CBDC)** suggest that the Federal Reserve is already exploring ways to modernize the dollar and prevent its displacement by digital alternatives, including China's e-CNY.

The U.S. can also leverage its established financial and geopolitical alliances to counteract China's efforts. By strengthening multilateral trade agreements with countries that remain committed to the dollar, such as Japan, South Korea, and key European partners, the U.S. can build a bulwark against China's currency ambitions. Moreover, diplomatic efforts to ensure that oil-producing nations in the Middle East continue to use the dollar for energy transactions could help preserve the petrodollar system, which remains a critical pillar of dollar dominance.

### 3.4. The Role of Global Institutions

Global financial institutions such as the **International Monetary Fund (IMF)** and the **World Bank** also play a pivotal role in maintaining the current financial order. While China has sought to increase its influence within these institutions, they remain largely structured around U.S. and Western interests. The Special Drawing Rights (SDR), the IMF's reserve asset, is still primarily backed by the dollar, even though the yuan was added to the SDR basket in 2016. However, China's long-term goal is to increase the role of the yuan in global reserve assets, possibly seeking a larger share of the SDR allocation.

China has also worked to create parallel institutions such as the **Asian Infrastructure Investment Bank (AIIB)** and the **New Development Bank (NDB)**, which is sometimes referred to as the BRICS bank. These institutions aim to provide an alternative to Western-led financial institutions and could be used to promote the yuan in infrastructure projects and other international investments. The success of these institutions will be a key factor in determining how effectively China can challenge the current global financial architecture and promote its currency for international use.

### 4. The Future of the Yuan and the Dollar: A Global Power Struggle

As China intensifies its efforts to position the yuan as an alternative to the U.S. dollar, the world could witness significant economic and geopolitical shifts. The competition centres on key areas, such as technological innovation, international trade influence, and strategic financial alliances. The dollar has long held the status of the world's reserve currency, but China's economic rise and increasing technological capabilities may challenge this supremacy. The analysis considers how digital currencies, central bank policies, and global investment flows could reshape this financial landscape, creating potential scenarios of either coexistence or dominance by one currency.

### Conclusion:

The future of the yuan and the dollar will be determined by a combination of technological advancement, political stability, and economic policy. While the dollar's entrenched position in the global system provides it with inherent advantages, China's rise as a major economic power and its focus on innovations such as digital currencies could challenge this status quo. However, significant obstacles, such as market trust in the yuan and China's ability to maintain openness in its financial systems, may impede the yuan's global ascendancy. Ultimately, the global power struggle between these two currencies will likely shape not only financial markets but also the broader geopolitical order for decades to come.

# Epilogue

As I conclude this work, I find myself reflecting on the intricate and often perilous dynamics explored within these pages. For over 40 years, I have immersed myself in the study of Chinese antiques and dynasties—a passion that has afforded me a unique perspective on China's long history and its cultural foundations. This deep engagement with China's past has sharpened my understanding of its present ambitions and informed my analysis of the country's aspirations on the global stage.

China's rise to prominence in the modern era is not an isolated phenomenon but rather the continuation of a narrative that stretches back millennia. Each dynasty, with its ambitions, struggles, and conquests, has contributed to a legacy of strategic brilliance and unyielding resilience. The Communist Party, much like the dynasties of old, has positioned itself as the architect of a new China, one that seeks to reclaim its historical role as the dominant force in world affairs. But this new era, as I have explored, comes with unprecedented challenges and risks for both China and the global community.

Through the lens of history, I see parallels between China's past and its current gambit for global dominance. This nation, forged in revolution and sustained by meticulous statecraft, has always valued patience and long-term strategy. Today, as it challenges the West in areas ranging from military power to economic influence, the stakes have never been higher. The Taiwan question, the South China Sea disputes, and China's efforts to weaken its adversaries indirectly are all parts of this larger, calculated game that could reshape the future of global geopolitics.

For those in the West, it is essential not only to recognize these strategies but also to anticipate them. The theft of technology, the manipulation of global markets, and the pursuit of new alliances with Russia, North Korea, and Iran are tactics that echo China's historical manoeuvrings. Understanding these moves within the broader context of Chinese history reveals that while the methods may be modern, the motivations are deeply rooted in the country's past.

As I've outlined throughout this book, the West is not powerless in this struggle. I believe there are many opportunities to counter China's ambitions by leveraging its vulnerabilities, particularly its economic fragility and dependence on energy imports. By drawing on historical lessons and adapting our strategies, we can meet China's challenge on an equal footing.

In writing *The Dragon's Gambit*, I have sought to provide more than a simple analysis of modern geopolitical events. My goal has been to convey a deeper understanding of how history informs China's actions today, and what that means for the future of global power dynamics. The West's response to China's ambitions will shape not just the coming decades but the course of history itself.

My decades-long fascination with China's history and culture has left me with a profound respect for its people, its traditions, and its remarkable endurance. But it has also taught me that the same strengths that have propelled China through its dynasties can just as easily lead to its undoing. The question that remains is whether the West is prepared to meet China's calculated moves with strategies of its own, or if, like so many before, it will be caught off guard by the dragon's gambit.

John Shenton

The End

# Don't miss out!

Visit the website below and you can sign up to receive emails whenever John Shenton publishes a new book. There's no charge and no obligation.

https://books2read.com/r/B-A-RJUO-VTEAF

**BOOKS2READ**

Connecting independent readers to independent writers.

# Also by John Shenton

Business Plan Basics
The Bahamas - More Islands and Recipes Than You Expect!
Collected Musings from Bricks and Mortar to E-commerce
The Smart City Odyssey: Unveiling the Secrets to Traveller-Centric
Software
The Dragon's Gambit: China's Bid for Global Dominance and the
Western Response
Silent Weapon
Business Basics: Money Sources
Influx
Fried Chips
Mandates, Motors, and Misinformation
Echos of Orwell
Control and Chaos

# About the Author

John Shenton was born in Birmingham, England and grew up in postwar England. He spent several years as a Radio Officer onboard a variety of vessels sailing to the Persian Gulf, the Indian Ocean and South China seas.

With degrees and a background in electronics and computers he has lived and worked within the United Kingdom, Germany, Switzerland and Canada.

While doing so, he established numerous trading relationships in Japan, Korea, the USA, China and other countries.

He has been retired for some time now living in Montréal Canada enjoying golfing, sailing and many other things automotive.

# About the Publisher

By John Shenton

www.ingramcontent.com/pod-product-compliance
Lightning Source LLC
Chambersburg PA
CBHW051436150726
48000CB00005B/2132